THE FIRST BOOK

OF

MICHAEL

Syl Mortilla

First published 2015

The First Book of Michael

By Syl Mortilla

Published by Syl Mortilla at Smashwords

Copyright © Syl Mortilla 2015

The right of Syl Mortilla to be identified as Author of this Work has been asserted by him in accordance with the Copyright, Designs and Patents Act 1988.

This book is sold subject to the condition that it shall not, by way of trade or otherwise, be lent, resold, hired out, or otherwise circulated without the publisher's prior consent in any form of binding or cover other than that in which it is published and without a similar condition including this condition being imposed on the subsequent purchaser.

All rights reserved.

Cover design by Samar Habib

Photo by Harrison Funk ©2014 - All Rights Reserved.

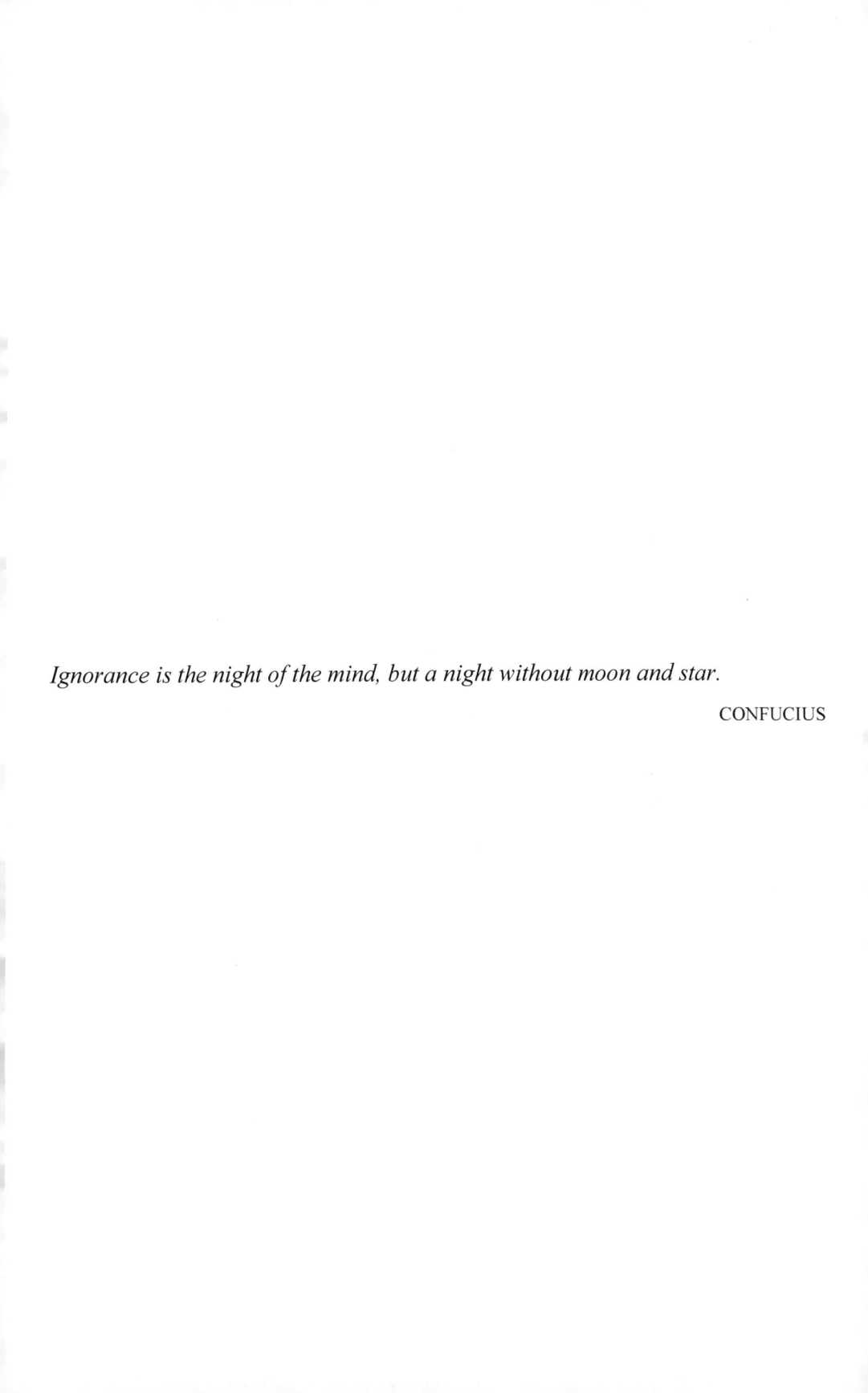

Ignorance is the night of the mind, but a night without moon and star.

CONFUCIUS

CONTENTS

Author's Note   1

Preface   4

Foreword   6

Introduction: *Dance first. Think later. It's the natural order.*   8

Chapter One: *All progress depends on the unreasonable man.*   18

Chapter Two: *Even a man who is pure of heart.*   54

Chapter Three: *Show me a hero and I will write you a tragedy.*   73

Chapter Four: *For the lips of a strange woman drop as a honeycomb.*   106

Chapter Five: *I, while living, have conquered the universe.*   125

Chapter Six: *His joyful vision is like an inner, immeasurable sorrow.*   159

Chapter Seven: *Proof that God has not yet given up on human beings.*   176

Chapter Eight: *The moon lives in the lining of your skin.*   202

Afterword   229

Acknowledgements   230

AUTHOR'S NOTE

The name 'Syl Mortilla' is an alias. The reasons for my employing a pseudonym are threefold: one is to protect my security; another is to grant me the liberty – perhaps paradoxically – to be myself; whilst the third – the one I consider most important – is because the name is an anagram of my mother's maiden name and my father's surname. My parents separated when I was a young boy; around the time that I discovered Michael.

The sobriquet 'Syl Mortilla', therefore, is primarily a statement of unity, one empowered by the magic of Michael's ability to heal.

Such was Michael's universal reach, it follows that a whole spectrum of personalities admire him. Ergo, the Michael Jackson fan community is comprised of many factions consisting of like-minded people who have interpreted Michael in their own particular way. Perhaps the one thing that the many different groups can agree on, however, is the importance of his aspirational message of promoting understanding and peace.

I do not profess to be any kind of oracle on the life and soul of Michael. I understand that the opinions and theories I proffer in this book will not be appreciated by everyone; indeed, I'm keen to ignite debate. For far too long, the artistry of Michael has been constantly devalued by the vacuity of laziness and salacity.

The ethical compass of humanity has become maniacally awry; its map of morality in tatters. The world is devoid of a unifying totem. I want this book to be important. This book is my heart. My sole hopes for this book are that it contributes as a counterbalance to the perpetual undermining of a culturally crucial figure, whose career was motivated and galvanised by historically unprecedented efforts of philanthropy and humanitarianism; and that at its conclusion, the reader is left in no doubt with regards the magnitude of respect and love that I possess for Michael.

For Michael.

PREFACE

He knew her intimately for nearly thirty years. During this time, she was his confidante, his protector, and his advisor. She rubbed cream into the piebald patchwork that was his back and shoulders: a torso that no-one else got to view, unless she had applied concealing make-up beforehand. He was very insecure about his vitiligo. He was very insecure about his overall physique. During times of stress, he would often fast to feel better about himself – often miss meals, try to concentrate instead on making his work as perfect as possible. Fasting and exhaustion landed him in hospital on numerous occasions. Stress exacerbates the effects of vitiligo. She tried to ensure he was fed.

His face was pocked with acne scars. He believed his nostrils were vast, his chin not clearly defined – that it seemed to get swallowed up by his neck. He was self-conscious about his smile. But he liked his eyes. He would ask her to accentuate them. He had his eyebrows tattooed on. And his lipstick. It saved a lot of time. And meant that when she wasn't around, they remained there – indelible swooshes of self-esteem reassuring him from the mirror. A lifetime in the public eye had taken its toll. The camera was his nemesis. He would wear a surgical mask, or hide behind strategically straggled curls and a fedora – unless she had primed his confidence first. She did this by combining her artistic skill with a unique, nuanced knowledge of the intricacies of his face, as well as an inimitable understanding of how he liked to look – though she also knew that he was capricious in these matters. Such is the nature of insecurity. He was changeable in his choice of hairstyle – sometimes preferring more curls or body in his hair, which gave him a sense of having his face covered, like when he wore the mask. She created and fixed his wigs for him. For nearly thirty years.

Still. Since they had known each other for nearly a third of a century, she would have usually intuited his mood before he had even sat down in the chair. The chair in which they talked. The chair in which they cried together; laughed together. The chair in which they would put the world to rights. For nearly thirty years. Some are jealous of the intimacy they shared. After all, their relationship was both as open and as close as any can be. She knew and understood his secrets, his intentions, his vices, his desires.

He trusted her. Implicitly. She prepared him for his final corporeal resting place. His deathbed.

He was Michael Jackson. And she was Karen Faye.

FOREWORD

Syl Mortilla was a Twitter presence that appeared on my timeline, intriguing me to tap on the bold typeface, and see what this mysterious blog had to say. After Michael Jackson died, I often hesitated to read or listen to what others opined about the iconic entertainer, who over the years became more like a brother to me. Most of what so-called insiders had to share was judgmentally unrecognisable, profit-driven journalistic nonsense, about the man I grew to know. Most often I decide not to waste my time reading "disclosures" inspired by a paycheck or notoriety.

Michael and I were young, innocent and ambitious when we first met. Our lives intersected - destined in space and time – on a photo shoot in Culver City, California. That day turned into us sharing some of the most magical and tragic times of our lives. Unbeknownst to me, at that first meeting, was just how many spirits all over the world Michael would touch in so many deep and meaningful ways.

I have responded to many questions since 2009, hoping to spread truth to those people Michael cared so dearly about - his beloved fans. So much that has been written is contrary to what I learned about Michael over the twenty-seven years we shared together.

When I clicked on Syl's blog, I actually cried when reading his insights. It brought me so much joy to find someone who heard

Michael's message so clearly, and could articulate it with the depth that Michael intended.

I am always touched by Syl's insights. Syl's writing opened up my own understanding of Michael's life - from a point of view other than my own - that rang true. Syl Mortilla's writing is the blood pulsing from Michael's heart to all of his fans. *The First Book of Michael* is a beautiful and honest contribution to the legacy of Michael Jackson, from a person who comprehends the messages Michael created, and left us to discover for all time.

I know everyone who has been touched by Michael will enjoy this book, and those that didn't understand Michael, will find clarity in Syl's writing.

Michael's life spoke, and Syl Mortilla was listening.

Karen Faye

December 2014

INTRODUCTION

Dance first. Think later. It's the natural order.

SAMUEL BECKETT

I can't remember the first time I tried to emulate Michael's dancing. It was possibly when I was seven – when, along with my siblings and some friends of ours, I tried to recreate the 'The Way You Make Me Feel' short film. Naturally, being the eldest sibling, I assumed the role of Michael, and the girl I fancied from down our street got chosen (at random, obviously) to play the role of the object of Michael's desire - the model Tatiana Thumbtzen (one of those beautiful ironies of existence that inclines me to believe in a parallel universe, is that these days, the real Tatiana follows me. Albeit, on Twitter - but I maintain it counts).

The ensuing years of my Michael-dancing self-education are a chronicle of excruciating memories involving mirrors, hairbrushes, failed crotch grabs, broken ornaments, and concerned expressions etched on the faces of my parents upon unfortunate bedroom interruptions. All with the added hindrance of my having been a rather overweight teenager.

However, the weight soon dropped off. Some teenagers play football; some swim; some play tennis. A rare few of us try to learn to dance like Michael. I became an addict. And I swear I encountered more spiritual experiences dancing to Michael's music than I had ever done in a thousand visits to church. The escapism. The losing oneself. Those special, special occasions, when - with hindsight after the rapture - it felt as if I had been doing nothing less than channelling the man himself.

Another - more orthodox - teenage hobby is learning to play an instrument. And there are certainly similarities between that past-time path and my own preferred weapon of choice. With a guitar, for example, one can entertain most people after having mastered a few basic chords. Yet as all musicians know, the devil is in the detail: in the intricacies of an instrument. Rudimentary choreography such as the "Too high to get over, too low to get under" routine from 'Wanna Be Startin' Somethin'', or the 'one-hand-in-your-pocket-whilst-the-other-hand-clicks-its-fingers-in-the-air-exactly-one-hundred-and-eighty-degrees-from-your-simultaneously-swinging-heel' move (you know, that one) are seen as impressive by people not in the know. But for true authenticity, those of us fully initiated understand that it's as much in the face as it is the limbs: in the frightened, imploring eyes;

the caught-by-surprise raised eyebrows and pout; and that apparently enraging part of the floor to be unflinchingly stared at – making you angry, perhaps, with its insisting you bite your bottom lip whilst your pelvis thrusts at a rate of ten-to-the-dozen (or 4/4, at least).

I competed with myself as to how many spins I could accomplish in one attempt - though, not just any old revolutions, mind. Spins in which you stop in perfect time, with a closed fist at the end of an arm outstretched in the chosen direction. Or a pointed finger, into which, as Michael instructs in the 'Jam' video, you "Put all your energy… and – fire!"

Whilst on the subject of hands - one mustn't neglect to mention the spontaneous fluttering of the index and middle fingers – a subconscious keeping of time with some silent, esoteric rhythm. Though the less said about this, the better. Especially when queried by schoolmates in classroom scenarios.

Incidentally, I am a firm advocate of the teaching of dance in schools. I believe dance should be incorporated within any pedagogical curriculum, and granted the same gravitas as literacy or mathematics. The practice of educating the limbs with rhythm is effortlessly absorbed by the soul, whereupon it is processed, before being expressed through the intellect. Just look at Michael. He evolved from the James Brown mimic into an innately, uniquely talented singer, songwriter, lyricist and poet. The vocal staccato rhythms he preferred - harnessed so spectacularly by *Off The Wall* and *Thriller* collaborator, Rod Temperton - were a direct extension of his predilection for dance. And has any human ever danced more than Michael did?

Of course - we all dance, all the time. We dance to the music of the spheres - to the frivolity or ferocity of the capricious winds; we dance in the enforced shuffle of our autumnal years, or the spritely spring in a step that announces our being newly in love; we dance in the everyday walk to the shop to buy milk and bread.

After directing the 'Jam' video - in which Michael and basketball legend Michael Jordan demonstrate their dominance in their chosen entertainment fields - David Kellogg mused,

"My takeaway was that I never saw basketball the same way since. Basketball players are just dancers running around in a choreographed and improvised routine with a prop, doing spectacular acrobatics before a large audience of pumped up fans."

'Pumped-up fans' who are also playing their part in the communal dance.

Though – admittedly - perceiving our every movement as part of a dance was perhaps easier for a man who interpreted the ambient sounds of a dripping tap, a sweeping brush and a struck match as a coalesced rhythm - as Michael so ingeniously exploited in his 'You Rock My World' short film.

You can't think about dancing as you do it, though. Like Michael said, "Thinking is the biggest mistake a dancer could make. You have to feel." You go with the flow. Exquisite dancing is executed in a vacant state of 'not-thinking'. With Michael's seeming direct link to something otherworldly, he knew instinctively how a routine should happen. 'Smooth Criminal', for example, where you simultaneously raise both arms and one knee one way, then mirror the move towards the other side. Well - it occurs to you - of course: it's meant to do that.

Yet, it's only once you have managed to absorb the routine that you appreciate the other genius advice Michael offered on dancing: that you unthinkingly allow the music to ordain you with the knowledge of how to move your limbs. You improvise around a framework; a routine.

One instance of this routine and improvisation working in tandem is in the 'Bad' short film. Michael has embodied the choreography to the extent that he can slip in and out of it at will, whilst remaining cohesive with the supporting dancers. This is what Michael Jackson fans that dance do - they improvise around a routine that Michael had divined.

As the man himself mused in 2001,

"I pretty much just get in a room and I start to dance... I don't create the dance, the dance creates itself, really. You know, I'll do something and I'll look back... I'll look back on tape and I'll go, "Wow," I didn't realise I had done that. It came out of the drums... Dancing is about interpretation. You become.... You become the accompaniment of the music. So when you become the bass of 'Billie Jean', I couldn't help but do the step that I was doing when the song first starts, because that's what it told me to do."

I suppose, then, that flawless dancing is perhaps less a product of 'not-thinking' and more one of 'faultless thinking' – a connection with a supremacy that streams thought silently through the body as pure action, with no middle-man to muddy the message.

Or, as the physician and writer Havelock Ellis stated, "To dance is to imitate the gods."

Michael reached levels of rapture in his dance that are reminiscent of Sufi Dervish dancing - his precision presenting us with a contemporary version of Hindu Mudras. The phenomenon of reaching transcendence through dance is well-documented. Spectators across history have borne witness to a performer's spontaneous transformation, whereupon the dancer would no longer appear to be merely human. And upon these occasions, the watchers would instinctively revere, appreciate and accept the experience for what it was - a glimpse of God.

In 2002, Michael said,

"...the same new miracle intervals and biological rhythms that sound out the architecture of my DNA also governs the movement of the stars. The same music governs the rhythm of the seasons; the pulse of our heartbeats; the migration of birds; the ebb and flow of ocean tides;

the cycles of growth; evolution and dissolution. It's music; it's rhythm. And my goal in life is to give to the world what I was lucky to receive: the ecstasy of divine union through my music and my dance... It's what I'm here for."

Following the *Brits '96* performance of 'Earth Song', fellow philanthropist Sir Bob Geldof introduced Michael to the stage, so that he could receive what Geldof described as the "one-off - like the man himself" *Artist of a Generation* award (albeit, "…what generation?" Geldof enquired, "…at least three have been listening to him already"). Geldof welcomed Michael using these words,

"...the most famous person on the planet, God help him… When Michael Jackson sings it is with the voice of angels. And when his feet move, you can see God dancing..."

Forum threads abound regarding the debate as to whether Michael was a better dancer or singer. It's a tough one. Michael could vocally emote like very few people to have ever existed, and his technical singing abilities - the whole gamut of them - were second to none. But for me, the magic is in the dance. As he promoted the *Bad* tour, Michael's then-manager, Frank Dileo, said that there were others who could sing as well as Michael, but no-one alive that could rival him for dance. And I'm inclined to agree. Michael himself, as he grew older, relied more and more on his moves rather than his voice. He felt most secure dancing. Which makes sense - I mean, how many iconic dance moves and routines can one man immortalise? It's an embarrassment of riches. He was truly extraordinary.

Naturally, Michael had his influences. He threw the various geniuses James Brown, Jackie Wilson, Gene Kelly, Bob Fosse, Charlie Chaplin, Marcel Marceau, Fred Astaire and Sammy Davis Junior into an alchemy pot (imagine that party), and came up with – well, you know: that molten-metal angel-alien we witnessed morphing across stages, with a dance that entranced human beings all over the globe.

'The Dance' (as Michael referred to it in his book, *Dancing the Dream*), was Michael's lifeline. Fred Astaire described him as "an angry dancer", and Michael - after suffering a uniquely oppressed childhood - did indeed have a great deal to be angry about. But just imagine what a better world we would live in if all rage was expressed like this?! In Michael's song 'Blood on the Dance Floor', it's not coincidental that such a contrast exists between the guttural vox of the verses and the orgasmically unleashed vocals of the bridge, with its ecstatically sung lyric, "To escape the world I got to enjoy that simple dance".

Dancing was how Michael meditated. Like he said, "Dancing is important, like laughing, to back off tension. Escapism ... it's just great".

And - as I intimated before - give me learning to dance like Michael over prayer or yoga anytime. As a teenager bullied at school, Michael gave me the refuge of his dance, and for this I shall be eternally grateful to him.

So, the years progressed, and I continued to try and honour my hero. Every opportunity I had, I'd show off the arsenal of moves I'd accumulated over the years.

I became a psychiatric nurse, with one of my initial placements being undertaken in a respite centre for people suffering with schizophrenia. As I did the early rounds one day, I observed one of the residents dancing in his room. I couldn't hear the music he was dancing to, as he was wearing headphones so as not to disturb anyone. I continued on my round, then returned to the office. Whereupon, the senior nurse asked me to report on what the residents had been doing. I told her all I had seen, at which point she instructed me to write in the care notes of the 'dancing resident' that I had witnessed peculiar behaviour.

I asked her what that had been.

I continue dancing to this day. I doubt I'll ever stop. I imagine I'll be putting on shows when I'm elderly and in a nursing home. Or at least dancing in the privacy of my own room (when my parents - finally - won't be able to intrude). The nurses will say I'm senile. I'll refer them to the man with schizophrenia I once worked with.

Prior to an evening out, dancing around the house is perhaps the most enjoyable part of the process - a ritualistic prescient for what will inevitably come to pass on some unsuspecting dance floor. It's a warm-up, a practice.

For what has got to be the best party trick in the world.

Got the point?

Good.

Let's dance.

CHAPTER ONE

The reasonable man adapts himself to the world: the unreasonable one persists in trying to adapt the world to himself. Therefore all progress depends on the unreasonable man.

GEORGE BERNARD SHAW

Michael's art comprises a third of the triumvirate of topics that people discuss about him. The others being his legal tribulations, and his face.

The last occasion I saw Michael's face in the flesh, someone had just hit him.

Precisely whereabouts upon Michael's person is open to dubiety, though AEG Executive Randy Phillips - a man instrumental in convincing Michael to become involved in the doomed *This Is It* venture – flagrantly acknowledges the occurrence of the physical assault in an email exposed in the legal courts, during the trial in which Michael's mother's attempted to garner the truth behind why her son had died. Phillips also freely admits, in the same email chain, that he screamed at Michael "so hard the walls were shaking". In a further email within the same conversation, Phillips remarks "we still have to get his nose on properly." Whether this concern was meant literally or facetiously isn't clear. Regardless, it appears that Michael was being bullied.

There exists a close-up photograph of Michael's face taken during the 'They Don't Care About Us' rehearsals for *This Is It*, which unarguably displays the image of an agonised human being. Yet, it was used to promote the posthumous movie's release – apparently as proof that Michael was "in shape". It has since been copyrighted – hence, limiting its distribution. *This Is It* was an empty hearse. *This Is It* was nothing less than an international snuff movie that took cynical advantage of Michael's unrivalled levels of fame in order to rake in the dollars.

Randy Phillips had hit an evidently terrified and extremely vulnerable man. A man once worth billions of dollars, who had somehow found himself so heavily in debt that he had no option but to obey orders; a man that merely wanted to be able to afford a house for his children to live in; a man that had been whipped into shape to entertain an insatiable public since he was just five years old.

Michael's face was talked about a lot that week of the *O2* appearance. The press conference announcing his much-anticipated return to the stage provided the media with all the pictures they needed to satisfy their perennial 'count-and-compare' cosmetic surgery feature quotas.

***

The story goes that Michael's first taste of rhinoplasty was as a result of an accident on stage during 1979's *Destiny* tour, when Michael was twenty-one years old. This may well be true. However, it was also around this time that Michael wrote a recently unearthed motivational guidance note to himself, in which he stated,

"MJ will be my new name... I want a whole new character, a whole new look. I should be a totally different person. People should never think of me as the kid who sang 'ABC', 'I Want You Back'. I should be a new, incredible actor/singer/dancer that will shock the world."

Theories abound behind why Michael would want to alter his face as drastically as he did, with the most popular one being that he suffered with the psychological condition Body Dysmorphic Disorder, as a result of his having been the most photographed child on Earth. However - by his early twenties, Michael had already conquered the world. Maybe he then wanted to conquer it as someone else.

Michael began drawing pictures of elfin faces next to photographs of himself with the number '1998' next to it (a good example is in his autobiography, *Moonwalk*). And, although it's true that Michael would sign many things with the curiosity-stoking '1998', it holds a certain poignancy when viewed with hindsight alongside these seeming future self-portraits.

Perhaps there swirled a perfect storm of ambition, enforced rhinoplasty and the onset of the pigment-destroying disease vitiligo. Perhaps it was borne as a logical consequence of an insecure, innate perfectionist who had spent decades of his life rehearsing in front of mirrors. Perhaps Michael embraced and harnessed this tempest to create and control his Barnum-esque whirlwind. The transformation became a double-edged sword, however: it helped sate his desire for a cemented and easily recollected place in the memory of infinity - but at what price for his public palatability? Though the inherent irony of the backlash against the mutable complexion and shape of Michael's face, is that he did more to benefit race relations than anyone else in human history. Well, him and his friend Madiba Mandela.

***

The final days of Mandela were a familiar circus to those of us all-too au fait with the mechanics of the parasitic press; with their orgy of audacity and mendacity in their slavering anticipation of the corporeal death of a hero. Hundreds of people - comprised of fans, media and the merely curious - gathered outside a building, chanting a man's name: singing for him, holding vigils, whilst the man inside the building suffered. As the great man's granddaughter, Ndileka Mandela, put it, "[They] want a pound of flesh. In the absence of facts, [they] speculate."

Thankfully, not all of the comparisons between Madiba and Michael are so painful.

Pictures of meetings between Michael and Mandela portray two bona fide heroes in enthusiastic embrace: brothers in arms. Imagine the charge in that room? Perhaps the most telling example of the bond between the two benevolent behemoths, however, is the quote from President Mandela describing Michael as "a close member of our family." Michael reciprocated this love during the 2005 child molestation trial, with the words: "Mandela's story is giving me a lot of strength".

The colossal cultural strides that these men took, bridged gaps between religious and political differences; they stood as flaming torches amongst humanity: their fuel of humility starkly illuminating the darkness of jealousy - a jealousy manifest through their being globally slandered as miscreants. As Mr. Mandela stated, "The path of those who preach love, and not hatred, is not easy. They often have to wear a crown of thorns." The two men were uniquely civilised human beings – evolutionary cusps, perhaps evidencing better than anything else an eventual spiritual progression for humanity. They invited us to celebrate the ecstasy of diversity; they personified Goethe's poetic claim that "Colours are light's suffering and joy". If they were terrorists, they were terrorists of love.

There is a historical poignancy in these men dying in such close chronological proximity to each other. Signs of their time. The annual commemorations will be desperately and appropriately sad: morose celebrations of the life of the humanitarian entertainer stirring an emotive groundswell in preparation for the celebrations later that year of the life of the humanitarian politician - two giants among men that stood steadfast in the face of violent adversity, in their perceived-as-idealistic beliefs in peace. But handcuffed with this grief, must be the recognition that upon these two dates every year, our collective mass of mutual understanding evolves and multiplies exponentially.

There was always such contradiction in the backlash against Michael's change in skin colour. Yet, as a statement from the Vatican upon his death put it, his "surgeries elicited a personal rather than ethnic redefinition." After all, Michael ultimately became of almost translucent - rather than of white Caucasian - appearance: a translucence that transcended barriers imposed by racial identity.

The philosophies of Nelson Mandela and Michael can be our global antidote to cynicism. They taught us that there is no weapon as abundant or as robust as love, and that the good fight is worth fighting for. They taught us all to be brothers in arms.

***

The turbulence and brutality of the world and its press empires that were prejudiced against Michael manifested in his creating his home of Neverland. It is where he sought refuge. Though this is not to say that Michael shied away from conflict. On the contrary, Michael possessed an admirable courage to confront, yet preferring to do so using peaceful means. Indeed, any examples of Michael's arrogance were always borne of a reaction to his being treated unjustly: the *HIStory* statue that was floated down the Thames; the persistence in surrounding himself with children; the ever-increasing size of his white socks. Cornered animals seek to make themselves appear bigger.

In response to the attempt to have his freedom taken from him, Michael chose the recently Communist countries of Eastern Europe as a foundation for the *HIStory* campaign. He opted to promote freedom through the portrayal of his stark individualism, in countries entrenched in the active homogenisation of its people by their governments. With the irony being Michael's demeanour expressing a homogenisation of so many cultural differences: an embodiment of universality traversing not only the boundaries of race and gender, but also of age.

Michael implored us to "harmonise all around the world". His philosophy for a successful society appeared to be one that is celebratory of each person's individuality, with the primary motivation of each individual being the potentiation of their fellow human being through means of reciprocated assistance, and the acceptance of the unbridled freedom of each individual to achieve this.

That - in the mirror of each individual, society finds its reflection.

***

To say Michael was a liberal is perhaps an obvious statement. Yet as with most people, there existed elements of his persona which didn't comfortably fit within this moniker. One particular area in which Michael wouldn't typically be identified as a 'liberal' is in the issue of foetal abortion, something he was quite clearly opposed to in his song 'Abortion Papers', in which he sings, "Those abortion papers / Signed in your name against the word of God / Think about life / I'd like to have my child".

Although – conversely - in the *Thriller* track 'Wanna Be Startin' Somethin'', Michael unapologetically states, "Don't have a baby, if you can't feed your baby". Perhaps Michael was liberal to the militant point of acknowledging the right to freedom for foetuses, as opposed to the freedom of the mother and father that conceived them. This would make sense, considering his adoration of children and ideology of fulfilling potential.

During the eighties and early nineties, Michael was twice entertained at the White House by the *Republican Party* (though this may well have been mere opportunism by the presidents in question: they had the chance to meet Michael - and they took it). However, although content to be entertained by the Republicans for reasons of self-promotion, it was the Democrats for whom Michael opted to actively entertain and raise funds for.

And Michael's private behaviour was certainly not conducive with the eighties mantra of greed and excess, what with his record-breaking philanthropic ventures and penchant for purchasing from charity shops. This was a trait that had been instilled in him since his poverty-stricken childhood, and one of the many behaviours inherited from his stoic but gentle mother, Katherine. As part of the riposte to the public relations catastrophe that was the Martin Bashir interview, *Living With Michael Jackson*, Michael released his *Private Home Movies* documentary. It was a collection of candid footage of him over the years. One segment shows a *Thriller*-era Michael being filmed in a car on the way to Alabama with his brothers, in which, after his suggestion that they pay a visit to the *Salvation Army*, Michael is endearingly forced to defend his predilection for a bargain, arguing,

"…don't laugh. You find good stuff… That other places would sell real expensive… I'm tellin' ya… You gonna be hittin' them soon when the depression hits ya."

Michael's contemporaneous musical peer, Prince - on the other hand - was a screaming true blue, as evidenced on his *Around The World In A Day* album, on which he sings, "Whoever said that elephants were stronger than mules?" I like to imagine an agenda at one of the two great pop artists' many clandestine meetings (one of these occasions at least occurring over a game of Ping-Pong), involving a conversation in which they decided to separate the two political polarities of the time – the communist and the capitalist – and schemed to work in cahoots in promulgating a message of universal peace. After all, there was a mutual admiration between them, with both paying tribute to each other's work: Prince's covers of 'Don't Stop 'Til You Get Enough' (original percussion on the record courtesy of longtime Prince collaborator, Sheila E) and 'Shake Your Body (Down To The Ground)' occasionally feature in his concert set-lists; whilst Michael paid homage to Prince by using his music in the band intermission on the *Bad* tour, as well as incorporating the refrain "Let's work!" - from Prince's track of the same name - into some live versions of the 'Billie Jean' dance breakdown. In *Moonwalker*, there is a joke about Michael's chimpanzee Bubbles choosing to wear a Prince T-shirt.

Michael's response to the 1993 allegations was a lesson in socialist propaganda: the robot from *Moonwalker*, fresh from annihilating hundreds of faceless clones, mutated into the Stalin-esque *HIStory* statue; the teaser for the associated album was a direct lift of Hitler's *Triumph Of The Will*; the 'Earth Song' video was clearly influenced by the 1972 Soviet propaganda video, *Ave Maria*; the spoken outro to 'Stranger In Moscow' translates as "Why have you come from the West? Confess! To steal the great achievements of the people, the accomplishments of the workers."

Michael had much more to do with the fall of the Berlin wall than anyone had ever thought. The Stasi were so worried about his influence that they ran a covert operation on him during his visit. Notes in a file created by the East German secret police describe how Michael had been watched as he toured Berlin. The Stasi spied on his visit to the Berlin East / West border checkpoint, observing that:

"three cars pulled up to the border crossing, with many unknown male and female people. Among the people was the USA rock singer Michael Jackson. Accompanying him at all times was a female person, about 25 years old, 165 centimetres tall, with a slim build."

Namely, Karen Faye.

The Stasi were concerned that the *Bad* tour concert Michael gave in Berlin in June of 1988 – a little over a year before the wall fell - would act as a catalyst for an already increasing level of disestablishment behaviour. The secret police worried that the "youths will do anything they can to experience this concert, in the area around the Brandenburg Gate… youths are planning to provoke a confrontation with police." The amount of foreign media that would be present for the concert flagged the situation up as a potential national security threat.

It was common knowledge that Michael was performing in front of the Reichstag that evening, a mere few hundred metres from where the crowd had assembled. Thousands of young people congregated to hear him. Violent clashes between East German youths and police ensued.

The *HIStory* tour performance of 'Black or White' celebrates the fall of the wall, its climax featuring the destruction and collapse of a symbolic wall of speakers. 'Earth Song' on the same tour incorporates a tank rolling onto the stage at its conclusion. The significance of these visual symbols for the audiences in Eastern Europe, considering the contemporaneous events of that region, cannot be understated.

***

And lest we forget the controversy surrounding 'They Don't Care About Us'.

Michael's use of the words 'Jew' and 'Kike' in 'They Don't Care About Us' resulted in his being forced by Sony Music to mask the offending terms. Which he did by utilising what was tantamount to a sonic scribbling out. And in the very act of making these alterations so obvious, he managed to explicitly express his disgust at the enforced censorship. Footage shot during the recording of 'They Don't Care About Us' shows a silhouetted Michael angrily throwing equipment around a studio. Ensuing variations of the track – released on later compilations – replaced the 'trashing' sound Michael had cut over the censored words, with an equally auditory jarring repetition of the lyrically arrhythmic word from the first part of the line – "Kick me, *kick* me / Don't you black or *white* me." The song is thus forever both scarred and sanctified by this intentional lack of proper rectification. Or – to paraphrase Michael's adlib at the denouement of said track – "it's there to remind us."

During the Diane Sawyer interview that Michael organised in order to promote the *HIStory* album, the "vainglorious" *HIStory* short film was shown. It is a work that irrefutably borrows heavily from the Nazi propaganda piece, *Triumph of the Will*. As part of this interview, Michael defends his use of the terms 'Jew' and 'Kike' in 'They Don't Care About Us' with the retort that he was merely utilising the imagery to illustrate the extent to which he himself had become a victim. As in, how Jewish people were victims when subjugated by the atrocities meted out upon them during the Holocaust. Indeed, the word 'Kike' is derived from the Hebrew word for 'circle' – a derisory term given to Jewish immigrants as a result of their being required to draw a circle on themselves instead of a cross, upon their arrival in America after fleeing World War II atrocities.

And – certainly – Michael had also been marked and victimised.

In conversation with Rabbi Schmuley Boteach, Michael argued,

"Well I'd say, they don't care about us, those who are treated unjustly, those who have been bastardised, being called '"nigger", being called the word that they misunderstood me for when I said those who say "kike" to people. When I was a little kid, Jews, we had Jewish lawyers and Jewish accountants and they slept in my bed next to me and they would call each other "kike". I said "What is that?' and they said, "That's the bad word for Jews. For blacks they say 'nigger'. I said "Ohhh." So I always knew when people have been bastardised, they've been called 'nigger', they've been called "kike". That's what I am saying and they used it. They took it all wrong. I would never… you know?"

And in his official statement rebuffing the allegations, said,

"The song, in fact, is about the pain of prejudice and hate, and is a way to draw attention to social and political problems. I am the voice of the accused and the attacked. I am the voice of everyone. I am the skinhead, I am the Jew, I am the Black man, I am the White man. I am not the one who was attacking… I am angry and outraged that I could be so misinterpreted."

Yet, insofar as far as being "a victim" is concerned, one cannot ignore Michael's stance on the criminal violence flaunted by the nuclear power state of Israel upon the displaced Palestinian people. A situation Michael laments in another *HIStory* track, 'Earth Song', with the words: "What about the Holy Land? / Torn apart by creed" and even more explicitly in his lyric: "God's a place for you / Oh, Palestine / I believe in you / Oh, Palestine, I will die for you".

Michael liked to highlight social injustice – wherever it was, and in whatever form it took. He shone the spotlight on instances of oppression. In fact, almost two decades prior to the furore forged by the deaths and social disharmony resultant of Brazil's efforts to host the 2014 *FIFA World Cup*, Michael had already strived to focus the world's attention on the injustice of the wealth divide there, by means of the 'They Don't Care About Us' short film ('Brazil Version' – in which he performs both the Black Panther salute and the Nazi goose step, and whilst singing the words "The government don't wanna see", strikes a Nazi-salute timed to coincide with the utterance of the word 'government'). Brazil's economic disparity is starkly illustrated in the opening sequence of the short film, as the statue of the Vatican-installed *Christ the Redeemer* pans into view. Omniscient and omnipotent, it towers dominantly over the ramshackle slums that cower in its shadow, as a Portuguese voice speaking over the footage implores, "Michael, eles nao ligam pra gente" ("Michael, they don't care about people").

Brazilian people represent the African diaspora, and Michael's choice to work with the Brazilian percussionist outfit, *Olodum*, for the Brazil version of the 'They Don't Care About Us' short film was indubitably a political one. The colours worn by *Olodum* are red, black, green, white and yellow. Combined, the colours symbolise 'the movement of Jah people' - as Bob Marley put it - with each colour conveying a significance: the red evocative of the blood spilled under sufferance; green portraying the rainforests of Africa; yellow signifying gold, for prosperity; black for the colour and pride of the people; with white being totemic of world peace.

The location of the actual video shoot also holds poignant historical gravitas. It was filmed in the province of Dona Marte in a favela called "Largo do Pelourinho" - the exact spot where centuries ago, slaves were whipped and tortured by their masters. Hence the name "Pelourinho", or "The Pillory".

By 1996, the favela had become a drug baron's dream. Claudia Silva – the press officer for Rio de Janeiro's tourist board – later exalted Michael's positive influence on the area by saying, "This process to make Dona Marta better started with Michael Jackson… There are no drug dealers anymore, and there's a massive social project. But all the attention started with Michael Jackson."

Olodum express the historical and ongoing oppression of the people in an ecstatic, artistic way. But the weight of their statement should not be underestimated, and neither should Michael's decision to align himself with them; nor the fact that responsibility for both of the songs' short films directorship was entrusted to Spike Lee, whose canon of work up to that point had exclusively been of a political nature.

The chorus chanted by the backing singers in the short film versions of the track sound a lot like they have been adapted to, "They don't really care about Mike."

During the aforementioned Sawyer interview, Michael says - in his defence at allegations of being antisemitic - that, "Some of my best friends are Jewish" – listing Steven Spielberg amongst them. This was in spite of the two men's recent falling out over a reneged deal concerning the fledgling *Dreamworks* venture, and despite Spielberg being the driving force behind the imposed alteration of the words 'Jew' and 'Kike' (claiming Michael had resurrected the latter term from practical extinction and brought it back into common usage). And as true as Michael's statement regarding Jewish friends may or may not have been – it's about as clichéd a statement as one can make in any defence against accusations of bigotry.

However, it's worth bearing in mind that Michael's genuine advocate Elizabeth Taylor was also Jewish, as is the mother of his two eldest children (as well as her employer – principal Dr. Feelgood, Dr. Klein). Too, for the violin element of another *HIStory* track, 'Little Susie', Michael borrowed the melody from 'Sunrise, Sunset' - a song from *Fiddler on the Roof*: a film celebrating Jewish people. The *Invincible* album itself was dedicated to Benjamin Hermansen - an Afro-Norwegian boy stabbed to death by a group of neo-Nazis in January 2001. Furthermore, Michael begins the very song 'They Don't Care About Us' with the words, "Skinhead, dead head" – which is a blatant and direct rebuttal of Neo-Nazism.

Other lyrics in 'They Don't Care About Us' include the ambiguous reference to being "In the suite / On the news" – words easily misconstrued as "Innocent / On the noose", and the use of the homonymous lyric 'black male / blackmail'. As part of the Chandler settlement agreement, Michael was prevented from using certain terminology with which he could directly vindicate himself, so this was his method for overcoming any potential legal backlash. Another ostensibly surreal lyric in 'They Don't Care About Us' is, "Everybody dog food." It's open to interpretation, of course, but 'dog' is another particularly derogatory term used against Jewish people.

Michael namechecks both Martin Luther and Roosevelt in 'They Don't Care About Us'. The only question is: which of the namesakes is he referencing? The other famous Martin Luther – the one preceding the celebrated black luminary – was a notorious antisemite who authored a book entitled *On the Jews and Their Lies*. And - whilst one of the two presidents that carried the surname of Roosevelt is revered as a unifier – the other remains under suspicion as being less than sympathetic towards the Jewish plight. These ambiguities are seemingly clarified in the 'Prison Version' of the 'They Don't Care About Us' short film (where an incarcerated Michael is portrayed as the vulnerable human being he was - sweating armpits and all) – in which the images incorporated are of the publicly palatable examples of the Martin Luther and Roosevelt namesakes.

As ever, Michael successfully courted controversy and demanded debate. Still. 'They Don't Care About Us' is track two on the *HIStory* album. 'This Time Around' is track four. On track four, he incorporates a word with just as contentious connotations: 'Nigger'. The media response? Not a squeak.

***

In Michael's autobiography, *Moonwalk,* he recalls an incident when the *Jackson 5* were being interviewed, with their answers being scrutinised by Motown coaches sensitive to subjects that could be considered controversial. A black interviewer attempted to garner their views on the civil rights movement, but the Motown public relations representatives refused to let the *Jackson 5* respond. Michael remembers how he and his brothers threw up the black power salute as they left the interview.

Michael grew up immersed in the social tumult generated by the assassinations of both Dr Martin Luther King Jr. and Malcolm X. His mentor was Stevie Wonder, of whom he said,

"That's why I love Stevie Wonder's biggest-selling album called *Songs in the Key of Life*. He has a song on that album called 'Black Man'... I just jumped up screaming when I heard that record because he's showing the world what the black man has done and what other races have done, and he balanced it beautifully by putting other races in there, what they have done. Then he brings out what the black man has done. Instead of naming it another thing, he named it 'Black Man'. That's what I loved about it....And that's the best way to bring about the truth, through song. And that's what I love about it."

A sixteen-year-old Michael, in 1974, even performed backing vocals on Stevie Wonder's anti-Nixon track, 'You Haven't Done Nothing'.

In the introduction to the dance sequence of the 'Black Or White' video, a background statue of notorious slaver US President George Washington, is poised as if guiding the black panther (which takes a moment to growl at the statue) into the pantheon where it shapeshifts into Michael, who is clad primarily in black - though sporting a white arm brace and a chain belt around his waist.

The ensuing dance in which Michael destroys racist graffiti sprayed on car and shop windows was construed as gratuitously violent by some. This led to Michael having to issue a statement in which he apologised for any upset caused and explained that he had merely been interpreting the instinct of a black panther. The dance sequence is shot in a street illuminated by hues on a spectrum from black to light blue. The black panther is the universally recognised symbol for the liberation of the black race. The official colours for the *Black Panther Party* (the original peaceful protest incarnation of the group, as opposed to the later militant offshoot), are black and light blue.

After the dance, Michael morphs back into a black panther, whereupon the final shot of the sequence is of the panther poised in an identical representation of the *Black Panther Party* logo. Michael would later incorporate the tail from this logo into his own 'MJ' emblem.

The political message in the 'Black Or White' short film is teased from the beginning. We start immersed in a point-of-view shot of some entity soaring through a night sky of black and blue, before it plunges through the clouds into a middle-America suburbia that has white-rock as its soundtrack. The entity seems to be searching for something to possess. It stalls for a double take on one particular house, before inviting itself in.

The perspective then alters to become a standard view. A fat, white American man and his blonde, petite wife sit in the lounge; the man is trying to watch a baseball game, though is evidently irritated by the noise of the loud music emanating from his son's bedroom upstairs. The man is eventually compelled to stomp upstairs and chastise the boy, demanding he "Turn that noise off!" On his way out, the man slams the door behind him, and a framed poster of Michael with his fist in the air during a *Bad* tour rendition of 'Beat It' falls to the floor with a smash. Out of vengeance, the boy then proceeds to construct an enormous speaker system in the living room. Once assembled, his distracted parents finally notice what their son's been doing (at which point - just to tantalise the next chapter – is it just me, or does the man commentating on the baseball match in the background really say "Satan"?). Having gotten his father's attention, the boy exclaims, "Eat this!" and plays a chord on his electric guitar - the noise from which blasts his portly father through the roof, and up into the moonlit black and blue sky. The fat, white man and his armchair then land in sub-Saharan Africa with a thud. Just in time to witness tribesmen hunting down a pack of imperious lions.

The ensuing 'pop' segment deconstructs the world's myriad ethnic dance stereotypes by pulling the camera away and exposing the artifice of each scene. It emphasises the delineation between the cultures of the world, yet simultaneously celebrates the possibilities of unifying the world through the medium of song and dance.

The upbeat melodies in 'Black Or White' (bar the bridge in which Michael furiously spits, "I ain't scared of no sheets" and where, in the short film, Ku Klux Klan imagery is engulfed by the flames he is bursting through (Michael had also incorporated Ku Klux Klan imagery in the video for 'Man In The Mirror', three years previously), are deceptive in the same manner that Michael's first self-penned track, 'Blues Away' (1976) also are - in which the lyrics concern heartbreak. The narrative of 'Black or White' tells the story of a mixed-race couple being questioned, with the black male protagonist being derogatorily labelled as "boy".

'Black Or White' was not the first time Michael had employed the term "boy" in such a way. The short film for the song 'Speed Demon' shows the black-voiced protagonist "heading for the border" before being told to "pull over, boy and get your ticket right" by a white cop. A cop who then instructs Michael that it's against the rules to dance (but demands an autograph from him anyway).

(As an aside supporting the idea of Michael always striving for precision in his art, it's interesting to note that the grammatically erroneous lyric from the 'Black Or White' rap, "I've seen the bright get duller" was corrected for live performances to "I've seen the sharp get duller".)

In response to the controversy evoked by the panther segment, one news anchor mused, "My guess is that it's Michael's childlike playfulness that got him into this problem, and his childlike openness that solved it."

It is a musing that takes on far greater gravitas when considered in the context of what was to happen in the ensuing months.

***

The follow-up single to 'Black Or White' was 'Remember The Time', directed by black film-maker John Singleton (another collaborator - along with Spike Lee - who worked on *Black Panther Party* films. Michael even provided the song 'On the Line' for Lee's film *Get on the Bus*, about the Million-man March).

Michael had previously approached Steven Spielberg about the possibility of making a movie about Ancient Egypt, using black actors. This was a bid by Michael to use Spielberg's influence on popular culture as a way of giving mass exposure to the magnificence of a time in human history when black people were the dominant race. Following Spielberg's rebuttal, Michael wrote and recorded the song 'Remember The Time' and sought Singleton to direct.

Michael's typical reaction to rejection was to counterpunch with a mightier force. Upon its release, the *Off The Wall* album was hailed by fans and critics alike as a milestone in musical history – a punctuation that encapsulated and defined the disco era of the 1970s. The subsequent failure of this consensus to be reflected in its award tallies inspired Michael to determine "They won't be able to ignore me next time". And sure enough, Michael's next visit to the *Grammy Awards* saw him leave with an unprecedented eight gongs (although it seems by the time of *Bad*, the establishment had had quite enough of this young upstart, with him then receiving a scandalous none). A sense of having been unfairly treated motivated Michael into reaching his commercial peak. Heartbreak fuelled Michael's success. 'Remember The Time' was dedicated to Michael's object of unreciprocated erotic love, Diana Ross, and it's easy to infer from the lyrics that she was the inspiration for the creation of the song. But here exists a duality between the song's muse and the short film's theme. Michael's propensity for generalising an idea was both ingenious and necessary.

During an interview between Michael and esteemed black rights activist Rev. Jesse Jackson, Michael spoke of the heritage of Africa being perennially and intentionally misrepresented; how history has attempted to separate Egypt from the rest of Africa, as though it's on another continent. Remember the time when Africans once ruled the world? Michael and John Singleton did. There are other references to Africa in the *Dangerous* campaign, such as the 'Heal The World' logo featuring a globe with a crack over Africa, and the globe basketball at the conclusion of the 'Jam' video, which a child picks up, with the continent of Africa facing the camera.

Spielberg did later take Michael's advice on making a film with black actors, however. It was called *Amistad*. And it was about African slaves.

The 'Remember The Time' short film had also been conceived as a response to the criticism of Michael's changing skin colour. As Michael promoted the *Dangerous* album, every country he visited ground to a halt upon his arrival; with the unparalleled extent of his fame providing him with a very real power to influence the hundreds of thousands of people he encountered. Every time Michael pounced on a stage during the *Dangerous* world tour - using what he called the 'toaster' - he did so to the sound of an attacking panther.

Within six months of the successes of the first two single releases from *Dangerous*, Michael began being ruthlessly pursued by a District Attorney mooted to be a member of the Ku Klux Klan. Though it was not until after Michael had had the gall to advertise the logo (an interracial shaking of hands) of the *Student Nonviolent Coordinating Committee* - a society founded by the leaders of black rights protests – during a 1993 *Superbowl* halftime performance that was viewed by hundreds of millions of people all over the world; and not until after Michael had disclosed an explanation for his changing skin tone as part of a record-breaking Oprah Winfrey interview – that the child molestation allegations against him were made public.

***

The monster that is the 'Thriller' short film means that Michael's other macabre magnum opus – 'Ghosts' – is often overshadowed by its older, colossal cousin. Nevertheless, the festival of Halloween always presents a cobwebbed window of opportunity for the less well-known of the two short films to shine. And although the 'Thriller' choreography may well be iconic - in comparison with the sophistication of its kindred cinematic spirit - its artistic significance has the mere pallor of the dead. 'Ghosts' is not only a spectacular visual and sonic treat – it is also politically-charged and multi-layered in its themes. Part of the choreography evokes the image of a hanging man.

Michael conceived 'Ghosts' as a response to the 1993 child molestation allegations. In the film, Michael plays the roles of a spectre, a skeleton, a demon, an oppressive village mayor, and a demonically-possessed version of said mayor. The aforementioned character played by George Wendt in the 'Black Or White' short film, meant we had already encountered one fat, white embodiment (and a substantial body at that) of the reactionary, radical capitalist mentality of Bible Belt (and a substantial belt at that) America. The mayor in 'Ghosts' was borne of a rather more specific muse, however - the late District Attorney Tom Sneddon.

It was perhaps fitting that at the hour of Tom Sneddon's death in 2014, many people across the world were continuing to celebrate the festival of Halloween – the time of year when many people believe that the boundary between the physical and the psychical realm is at its most permeable. Michael's song 'Thriller' and its accompanying short film are synonymous with the mischief of October 31st, its hand-in-glove theme and phenomenal success resulting in it now being universally accepted as the official anthem for the holiday.

The echelons of fame that the *Thriller* album vaulted Michael into contained two major drawbacks for him. Firstly, that he would forever be shackled with the impossible task of striving to improve upon the album's unprecedented commercial achievements; and secondly, that becoming the most famous person alive meant that the bounty on his head suddenly became dangerously high. Especially after his being shrewd and audacious enough to invest his capital into the white man's game of music publishing. A very young and uniquely influential black man suddenly became perceived by the establishment as one who was getting disconcertingly above his station.

The first inklings of political nuances in Michael's self-penned work began with the track 'Beat It' from *Thriller*. The political references are necessarily subtle – yet once you have interpreted the lyrics to 'Beat It' as concerning nothing less than the narrative of a lynching, it's hard to imagine the song as being about anything else. Consider the line "Don't wanna be a boy, you wanna be a man" as a simple reworking of the famous Malcolm X quote, "I ain't a boy! I'm a man!" Michael sampled Malcolm X for his 1995 track 'HIStory.' Consider that "The fire's in their eyes."

In 'D.S.' – the *HIStory* album diatribe directed towards Tom Sneddon – Michael labels Sneddon a 'BSTA'. This could be construed as an insinuation of the word 'bastard', but certainly as a play on the acronym 'SBDA', or 'Santa Barbara District Attorney'. The repetitive occultist chant that forms both the chorus as well as the denouement to the track dictates that "Tom Sneddon is a cold man". This mantra is finally terminated by the sound of a gunshot being fired. The start of the song features the unsettling sound of an angry, id-driven baby's cry.

Michael understood that millions of people around the globe would be chanting along with him to the chorus of 'D.S' – with him even taking the unusual step of including the track on the *HIStory* tour set-list. Michael had never before performed such an obscure album number on tour, but he brought out 'D.S.' to doubly ensure a communal chant of the ritualistic incantation. The song is shamelessly lip-synced, with Michael at one point handing over the microphone to a backing singer who is wearing an executioner's mask that completely covers his mouth. One desire of the 1993 extortionists was that Michael would "never sell another record." Michael was touring the world, performing in front of the largest crowds of his career, promoting the biggest selling double album of all time.

Sneddon had cynically and relentlessly attempted to systematically annihilate Michael. It was Sneddon's turn to be scared.

Tom Sneddon had written to the FBI asking them to convict Michael under the Mann Act – a law created in 1910 used to entrap boxer Jack Johnson in 1912 for what are now regarded as racially-motivated reasons. In spite of the LAPD having been enthusiastic about this line of enquiry in their pursuit of Michael, the FBI disagreed. Following his failure to bring Michael to trial as a result of the 1993 Chandler case, an unperturbed – or perhaps simply incensed – Sneddon then oversaw a successful change in the law that enabled him to resume his baseless chasing of Michael in 2005.

As part of this second wave of allegations, Neverland was stormed and ransacked. It was a strange, entirely fruitless act that involved hitherto unseen levels of scrutiny, undertaken by the ominous luminosity of metaphorical burning crosses; mob-rule insisting that the "freak circus freak" left the village. Michael had portentously referenced these events in the 'Ghosts' short film. And the last thing organised racists would do after carrying out a lynching such as that alluded to in the 'Beat It' lyrics? Seize the property of the lynched.

It's important not to elevate Sneddon as anything more than a footnote in the epic cultural event that was the life and career of Michael. However, it's an unfortunate and inescapable truth that the emotional agony suffered by Michael at the hands of the sinister Sneddon is what exacerbated Michael's use of analgesics as an emotional crutch.

There were many facets to Sneddon's malice: he was the relentless motor obsessed with maintaining the norm, repulsed by the myriad things his pitiful close-mindedness couldn't begin to comprehend; to Michael's celebration of imagination, Sneddon was the equivalent of the rote-learning of dead facts; to Michael's revelry in the ecstasy and infinity of rhythm, life and creation, Sneddon was the monotony of a drone engine seeking to destroy innocence.

And it was this engine that powered Sneddon's indefatigable, merciless hunt of Michael for over a decade. This trait of irrational tenacity was such an innate one of his, that it earned him the nickname 'Mad Dog' – a sobriquet Michael refers to with audible glee as he spits the words "Go'on you dawg, down boy!" during the adlibs of 'D.S.'

That dog is dead.

***

Michael understood that in order to fight bigotry and prejudice, he had to use his elevated position to capture the minds of children and turn them against the ingrained views of their parents. Which is why "Black Or White" begins with a boy standing up to his father.

The philosopher Friedrich Engels claimed the patriarchal family structure as the basic building block of capitalism: the father as owner, the wife as the means of production, and the offspring as the product. Both the means of production and product were the property of the patriarch. Michael, being black and belonging to the slave class of "the owned", was daring to steal their most precious of property - their children. As well as also hijacking the hearts of white women.

Another esteemed philosopher, Noam Chomsky, suggests the media's function is to "…amuse, entertain and inform, and to inculcate individuals with the values, beliefs and codes of behaviour that will integrate them into the institutional structures of the larger society."

Similarly, the film and music critic Armond White described the media as being "the superego of the status quo".

And this was another factor that generated the inordinate rage directed towards Michael during the 1993 allegations: the feeling that he was undermining the security of the patriarchal system; that he was somehow "stealing" children away from their fathers. Evan Chandler, the father of the 1993 accuser, even admits in his book that he was jealous of his son wanting to spend more time with Michael than him.

Evan Chandler was an estranged father insecure in his role, and felt threatened by the possibility of Michael replacing him.

Which is a natural reaction, albeit one borne of the more bestial elements of human nature – as all jealousy is. The more sinister and premeditated part of Evan Chandler's scheme, however, was the ruthless extortion attempt in which he was content with the idea of annihilating an innocent man. In truth, Michael did indeed steal the children from the orthodox patriarchy, and provided a new, non-patriarchal model; one exemplified by his later becoming both father and mother to his three children. Michael's reimagining of the family construct is often viewed as pathological, due to its non-conformity. As Michael said, "They don't understand it so it makes them feel very uncomfortable".

The traditional "loving family" does not need to be biological. As humanity is becoming more individualised, there is an evident increase in "tailored families" - tailored to maximise the potential for love.

***

On May 6th 1992, Michael anonymously covered the funeral expenses for Ramon Sanchez, a student killed by police during the

Los Angeles riots. The following year, Michael was subjugated to a humiliating strip search by the same LAPD.

Inspired by these events - and by the failure to bring to justice the LAPD police officers that were filmed murdering Rodney King - in 1995, Michael published the protest song 'They Don't Care About Us'.

'Scream- the first track and first single from the *HIStory* album also contains a reference to racism and police brutality. During the bridge, in the background, a radio broadcast reports, "A man has been brutally beaten to death by Police after being wrongly identified as a robbery suspect. The man was an eighteen-year old black male."

A revelation borne of the 2014 Sony emails hack exposes how 'They Don't Care About Us', prior to its publication, was purposefully dismissed and undermined by *New York Times* journalist Bernard Weinraub. The furore generated by Weinraub's description of Michael's entire *HIStory* album, which he described as "profane, obscure, angry and filled with rage" and of 'They Don't Care About Us' as containing "bigoted lyrics" meant that radio stations were reluctant to support Michael. The 'Prison Version' of the 'They Don't Care About Us' was banned in the United States.

Weinraub is the husband of Sony Pictures Chief Amy Pascal, who had previously been Vice President of Columbia Pictures, where Michael had had a movie contract that was never honoured. Pascal then became head of Sony Pictures. Weinraub also considered David

Geffen amongst his friends. Geffen being the man that chose Michael's management, as well as being in cahoots with Spielberg for the deception of Michael during the burgeoning *Dreamworks* venture.

On Twitter in December 2014, the hashtag #TheyDontCareAboutUs was trending globally, in reaction to the racially motivated unrest resulting from persisting police brutality in the United States. Michael's song was resurrected at the grass roots level in many cities across the United States. In Ferguson, the song could be heard emanating through car windows. In New York City and Berkeley, performances of the song formed part of the protests. The Morgan State University choir's contribution to the protests was a rendition of 'Heal The World'.

The integrity of the campaign group Ferguson Action - set up as a part of the protest movement - was reinforced with their statement in response to the death of two white police men killed by a mentally ill black man in an unrelated incident, that was seized upon by the media,

"We are shocked and saddened by the news of two NYPD officers killed today in Brooklyn. We mourned with the families of Eric Garner and Mike Brown who experienced unspeakable loss, and similarly our hearts go out to the families of these officers who are now experiencing that same grief. They deserve all of our prayers. Unfortunately, there have been attempts to draw misleading connections between this movement and today's tragic events.

Millions have stood together in acts of non-violent civil disobedience, one of the cornerstones of our democracy. It is irresponsible to draw connections between this movement and the actions of a troubled man...Today's events are a tragedy in their own right. To conflate them with the brave activism of millions of people across the country is nothing short of cheap political punditry."

Michael never forgot his humble beginnings, nor the suffering of black America. Indeed, a recent ancestor of his very own had himself been a slave: one named 'Prince' by his slavers. The same Prince that Michael named his white son after. The same son who stood trial as a plaintiff in the fight to get justice for his father, who died as a result of a slavish contract.

It may have taken twenty-five years for the minutiae of an event witnessed simultaneously by half a billion people - as well countless hundreds of millions since - to start being deciphered (as starkly obvious as they now seem), but with the 'Black Or White' short film, Michael further solidified his position as an artistic visionary. It was not merely that Michael had no other option but to convey his messages subtly, due to an awareness of the pitfalls he was doomed to succumb to; it was also that he remained fully cognisant of humanity's ongoing evolution of consciousness, and thus prepared his art within this context.

Much of Michael's art will take time to unravel and reveal its true significance; the messages will crystallise over time. The process of change is so often invisible to the naked eye: the weathering of a rock; the growth of a tree. Noticeable catalytic leaps are few and far between. The distance of hindsight is necessary.

As evidenced in the case of the hacked email scandal, and true to Michael's oft-quoted sentiment, "Lies run sprints, but the truth runs marathons", our persistence in exposing the truth of Michael - on many fronts - will eventually see justice realised.

With perhaps the most misunderstood and maliciously maligned example of this phenomenon, residing in Michael's philosophy of the genius of children and society's tragic dismissal of its usefulness.

CHAPTER TWO

Even a man who is pure of heart / And says his prayers by night / May become a wolf / When the wolfbane blooms / And the autumn moon is bright.

TRADITIONAL

Michael was a master marketeer. He adopted the renowned self-publicist PT Barnum as his public relations mentor, and learned to use Barnum's legendary tactics and abilities for his own self-promotion: the image of Barnum's head even appearing on the cover of the *Dangerous* album. Atop of this depiction of Barnum's head stands a 'midget ringmaster', who - in one of two *Dangerous* promos directed by David Lynch (the portent in that surname!) - would be played by *ALF* actor Mihaly "Michu" Meszaros, and hence join Emmanuel Lewis, the crew of *Captain Eo*, and Bubbles the chimpanzee on the ever-expanding list of Michael's diminutive circus friends.

Michael always knew how to work with the right people to convey the desired image. After working with A-list movie directors Landis, Scorsese, Lucas and Coppola in the eighties, Michael, through necessity, changed tack with the changing of the cultural winds. The self-manufactured eighties controversies of Merrick's bones and Hyperbaric Chamber had now evolved into the far more damaging issue of race-denial. Michael was now the tabloid press' Most Wanted. The swift and sudden fall of 1993 had not yet occurred, though Michael portentously alluded to its possibilities on the *Dangerous* album: both overtly in 'Will You Be There' and more indirectly in the 'Jam' lyric, "I'm conditioned by the system."

Michael's eminence in the sphere of self-promotion was unsurprising considering his upbringing. The *Jackson 5* had been used to advertise cereal, and his time with *The Jacksons* was what kick-started Michael's ill-fated, life-altering relationship with *Pepsi*: a partnership that began with adverts with his brothers and the *Pepsi*-sponsored *Victory* tour (during the 'Billie Jean' and 'Beat It' performances, Michael even wore a subliminally *Pepsi*-themed T-shirt). The joint venture continued for Michael's solo work, with *Pepsi* also sponsoring the *Bad* and *Dangerous* tours and projects. In response to the 1993 scandal, however, Michael was unceremoniously dumped by the company. Typically, Michael's riposte to being abandoned by his long-term marketing partners was a musical one. On the subsequent *HIStory* album, Michael placed 'Come Together' after the track

'Money'. 'Come Together' containing the lyric, "He shoot *Coca-Cola*".

The prosperous *Pepsi* partnership was rekindled by Michael's estate after his death.

The *HIStory* campaign was Michael's very personal retaliation to the molestation accusations, and for the first time, Michael profaned on record. A typically undermining critic of the time claimed Michael had started swearing to appeal to "the children of Cobain". In fact, Michael started cursing in his music because he was understandably and justifiably rather upset. (These persistent asinine attacks on Michael even stooped so low as one reviewer of the *HIStory* tour – which grossed as much as the *Bad* tour, with profits given to charity – claiming that Michael must have pushed a sock down the front of his trousers in order for him to have "achieved that bulge".) Michael also fought back with his message of environmentalism. 'Earth Song' was a phenomenal worldwide success (bar the out-of-favour USA, where it wasn't released), with Michael tapping into a universal anxiety concerning the welfare of the planet.

And then along came Jarvis Cocker: the historical footnote frontman for Britpop band, *Pulp*.

The day after Cocker's cynical stage invasion of Michael's performance of 'Earth Song' at *The Brits '96*, one newspaper headline read, "The Night Our Young Dreams Were Pulped".

This surprising message of media support for Michael was ephemeral, however. Once it had been noted that young and trendy Brits were not in agreement with the media stance, the backlash began. The following week, Cocker was interviewed on cult TV programme, *TFI Friday*. The programme contained a live audience of young adults, who mocked Michael and championed Cocker throughout. The host, Chris Evans, concluded the interview with the words, "We all support you and know it was just a bit of a laugh."

What it actually was, was a cultural watershed: a paradigm shift in the morality of a generation. Those children who had grown up entranced by Michael transforming into cars and robots in an effort to defeat a drug baron, suddenly became 'Cool Britannia' Blairites. But it was okay. At least they were all 'Sorted for E's and Wizz'.

A year previously, Chris Evans, who was also a *BBC Radio 1* DJ, had been the person to premiere 'Scream' on UK radio. After the song's unveiling- its opening lyric being, "Tired of injustice" - Evans immediately commenced a campaign to castrate the track: adamantly refusing to play the original version, insisting on the minimal playing of a remix (and not the 'Scream Louder' version, which incorporates the bassline from 'Thank You' by *Sly and the Family Stone* - one of Michael's favourite songs).

Upon the release of the *HIStory* album a few weeks later, Evans then proceeded to use his popular breakfast show to disproportionately slate Michael and the album. The subsequent success of the album and its singles ('You Are Not Alone' laying claim as the first ever song to debut at number one on the *Billboard* Charts; 'Earth Song' outselling 'Billie Jean' in the UK, with it holding the number one spot for seven weeks - including the much-coveted and hotly-contested Christmas Number One position), meant Evans then had to backtrack.

***

The *AEG* trial that exposed Randy Phillips' damning email correspondence, also revealed that if Michael had lived, he could have expected to earn over a billion dollars from the *This Is It* venture. The unprecedented demand for tickets to see *This Is It* meant - had Michael been physically capable of following orders - he would have eventually played to one million people. That's a tremendous amount of people representing a whole range of demographics who wanted to go and see Michael: a man who had essentially become a cult following during the noughties, having gone full-circle since the cult following of his band, the *Jackson 5* in the sixties. Before they exploded onto the world stage.

The day Michael died, the social network *Twitter* collapsed at 3:15pm, exact. Upon this internationally-sensed, seismic-shock, the resultant grief expressed by the planet at such an irreplaceable loss for humanity became manifest in myriad ways.

Conspiracy theories abound: had Michael known he was going to die when he did? When he had whooped the *This Is It* press-conference crowd into frenzied delirium with the chant, "This is it! This is it!" – had he literally meant *this - this moment* – is *it*? Conspiracy theories ranged from the ridiculous to the sublime: had Michael been targeted by secret *NASA* technology possessing the capacity to identify and exterminate any specific target on the globe – their motive being that, during the *This Is It* run of shows, they had reason to believe he was going to expose the insidious Illuminati elite?

Then there were those that point-blank refused to accept that he had died. A theory spawning a faction of fans who persevere in referring to themselves as 'BeLIEvers': a small group of seemingly sorry souls.

(I appreciate this could ostensibly be interpreted as an insensitive stance, but – from the BeLIEvers I've had the misfortune to encounter, at least – they promote their agenda for reasons much less fuelled by the denial synonymous with grief, and much more by one powered by necromaniacal voyeurism.)

BeLIEvers are inordinately proud of themselves for having noticed that, in the English language – on occasion – shorter words sometimes exist within longer ones (although the rudimentary rules of any language discourage those words ever being capitalised). This apparently startling syntactic revelation is the bedrock of the BeLIEver self-delusion system: an ethos that actively promulgates the idea of Michael being alive – with him merely residing on the sidelines of civilisation, in the guise of various individuals ranging from tragic burns victim and famous recipient of Michael's philanthropic aid, Dave Dave, to the very man convicted of killing Michael himself - Conrad Murray.

This lunatic fringe group put stock in such things as the reading of messages in the creases of the lips of the images of Michael that adorn posthumous album covers. The beyond-the-grave (nudge nudge, wink wink) messages vary; depending, of course, upon the native language of the interpreter.

BeLIEvers claim that the picture taken of Paris Jackson prior to her suicide attempt, in which she is sporting self-harm scars on her arm, was photoshopped - and that she is both aware of and complicit in perpetuating the hoax. Or else – with frightening contrariety – that Paris' attempt to take her own life was a ruse to draw Michael from hiding; that – for all Michael's self-defining concern for the welfare of other people's children – it's impossible for him to emerge from exile, and so simply refuses to intervene and console his own children in their agonised grief. Because the sanity of his kin must be duly sacrificed in lieu of the accomplishment of the bigger plan – a scheme of insidious deceit that essentially boils down to the most distasteful magic trick in history. The reveal to which, would be Michael's instant arrest and incarceration as a consequence of the somewhat misjudged endeavour being responsible for an innocent man having spent time in jail.

The voluntary acquiescence involved that allows oneself to hold such beliefs is not a symptom of grief; it is a result of purposeful self-perversion. And supporting such sentiments as these strikes at the very core of Michael's lived and hard-earned philosophy.

Fans of Elvis Presley that continued to insist on his persistent hip-thrusting upon this mortal coil, became a global laughing-stock (although their wordplay of ELVIS being an anagram of LIVES is actually far more credible – if only for the reason of it not having been randomly plucked from the ether as the term 'beLIEver' evidently was). However, the importance of their idol's legacy – compared to ours – pales in significance. Quite apart from the fact that Elvis fans didn't have to constantly contend with defending their idol against incessant accusations of paedophilia.

What with Michael's fans being all-too-often dismissed as deranged due to the actions of a loud, lunatic minority, Michael's vitally important message of kindness and brotherly love – particularly in the current global political climate – ends up becoming massively undermined. The lunacy plays directly into the hands of those wishing to smear his legacy. The BeLIEver movement represent a part of the integrity of Michael's art and soul that we must reclaim.

For the minority of BeLIEvers holding on out of genuine feelings of bereavement, perhaps they simply can't believe he's gone, because of course he's still here. Some things last forever. To live in the hearts and memories of those we leave behind is not to die, so in that sense Michael is surely more alive than any deceased person has ever been.

***

Considering the infinite permutations of perspective created by Michael's perfect storm: his level of fame; his being victimised; his own oracular propaganda technique of the dissemination of factoids; and the advent during this time of that supreme catalyst for suspicion, paranoia and unfounded hearsay – the Internet, it's hardly surprising that fans of Michael are so often daubed with the conspiracy theorist brush.

Michael's use of ambiguous imagery in the artwork for both the *Dangerous* and *Blood on the Dance Floor* albums provides a treasure chest for nuanced interpretation. The rational perspective is that these choices of cover artwork are merely an extension of the intentionally enigmatic promotional tactics utilised during the *Bad* campaign: such as the Elephant Man's bones and Hyperbaric Chamber controversies. Many others insist, however, that Michael had exorcised himself of such gimmickry with the release of *Dangerous*. Which therefore means Michael must have been attempting to use the imagery to covertly communicate the danger he was in: that the assembly line winding through the *Dangerous* album cover represents Michael's journey from Illuminati slave to Illuminati whistleblower; that Michael dancing on the checkered floor adorning the *Blood On The Dance Floor* cover represents his being emancipated from the role of Illuminati pawn.

Others argue that the 1997 *Blood on the Dance Floor* cover is portentous – that it is no coincidence that Michael's legs are positioned on the Manhattan skyline in situ of where the Twin Towers once stood, with his arms pointing to what would be the numbers 9 and 11 on a clock face. This interpretation is made further intriguing by the knowledge that Michael missed a meeting in the World Trade Centre on that fateful morning of 2001 – being late for the appointment due to over-sleeping after performing at his 30th Anniversary celebration concert, held at Madison Square Garden the previous night.

According to Illuminati observers, all the signs are that Michael became associated with this alleged egregious gang of elites just prior to making the *Thriller* album. Conspiracy theorists correlate Michael's increasing closeness to the *Disney Corporation* in the late seventies and early eighties with the rite of passage that - these days - is the *Disney Club* scholarship that all aspiring Satanists must now undertake. With Miley Cyrus being the most recent alumnus. Indeed, according to some conspiracy theorists, the song 'Thriller' - which was originally entitled 'Starlight' and themed on love, with lyrics including, "High in the night / This magic's gonna keep us close together / We'll start to fly / 'Cause this is the beginning of your life" - was turned into the occult-revering track 'Thriller' in order to satisfy a bargain with Satan: a deal in which Michael's fame was eternally guaranteed as a result of recording and performing the seminal soundtrack to the annual celebration of evil known as Halloween, and therefore being forever and inextricably linked with it. Decades later, and barely a *Disney* or *Dreamworks* animation goes by without the obligatory inclusion of the film's characters performing the 'Thriller' choreography as part of the DVD extras. Add all this to the stories involving the speakers exploding during Eddie Van Halen's recording of the 'Beat It' solo and of Michael's snake, Muscles, making itself at home on the mixing desk during the album's production, and it's easy to see where such mythology derives from.

Elite-terrorised conspiracy theorists scour the Internet for evidence of ritualistic acts that they believe are precursors to celebrity sacrifice. They contend that such events are practice-runs, one instance being the model made of Amy Winehouse before she died, in which she is pictured in a pool of blood, holding a Minnie Mouse mask. They point to the 'Thriller' short film itself, in which Michael is killed, as being his version of this. (Of course, Michael is also then reanimated in the video – the theme of resurrection a recurrent theme in his work, occurring as it does in both *Moonwalker* and *Ghosts*. But far be it from me to provide the BeLIEvers with any further ammunition). Famously, to appease the Jehovah's Witness movement, of which Michael was an active member, he was forced to precurse the 'Thriller' video with a disclaimer (actually penned by its director, John Landis) stating that the short film in no way endorsed a belief in the occult. Michael performed 'Thriller' right up to - quite literally - his dying day.

Awards shows appear to be most popular with Illuminati interpreters. No international award show goes by without its accompanying YouTube video pointing out the all-seeing-eye subliminally worked into a stage consisting of a suspiciously pyramidal construct. Pyramids, diamonds, and celebrities covering one eye, or using the Baphomet (devil horns) hand sign are like red flags to conspiracy theorists. Any celebrity referring to any of these themes is immediately fingered as a victim of mind control, a mere puppet performing a bit-role in the Elite's masterplan of creating the perfect welcome party for the coming of the antichrist and the ideal culture for his apocalyptic endgame. And it's true that these ostensibly incongruous motifs are inordinately alluded to in recent popular culture (Frank Ocean's 'Pyramids', Rihanna's 'Diamonds' and Beyonce's *Superbowl* Illuminati gesture, to note but three examples from 2013), although I imagine that's a lot more to do with the commercial advantages of playing up to Internet virality, rather than ritualistic acts of subservience to honour a taurine or strigine deity. Indeed, Michael himself was a prolific user of the Baphomet hand signal. And the original title for the song 'Liberian Girl' was 'Pyramid Girl'.

In spite of the 'Thriller' video disclaimer, rumours would persist. One story alleging that Michael hired the services of a witch doctor to enact revenge on Steven Spielberg, after the movie director's reneging on a deal involving Michael being a partner in the *Dreamworks SKG* enterprise (the company retained the use of the logo of the boy on the crescent moon that Michael had created as the emblem for Neverland).

***

The accumulated financial wealth of the richest eighty-five people on the planet, is more than that of the poorest three-and-a-half-billion people on the planet combined. It is this financial elite of people that are often the focal points for conspiracy theories. Even the Queen of England – by no means on the list of eighty-five – warned the late Princess Diana's butler with the words, "Be careful… No one has been as close to a member of my family as you have. There are forces at work in this country about which we have no knowledge. Do you understand?"

In this world divided between those struggling to make a living and those intent on limitlessly potentiating their already galactic financial situation, Michael was the shining example of the profligate philanthropist – giving more than three-hundred-million dollars to charity – with the will held by the Estate requesting a (still unsanctioned) bequest of a further twenty percent of his assets to good causes.

The image of PT Barnum's head on the front cover of the *Dangerous* album is often confused with that of renowned Satanist, Aleister Crowley. This mistake is either down to the malicious motivations of those that insist on promoting Michael as being something he wasn't, or another byproduct of Michael's self-concocted mist of mystery.

As for the cover of the *Dangerous* album – surely it is the most underrated of all time? Michael commissioned pop-surrealist artist Mark Ryden to create the image. It's an enigmatic masterpiece, one that reveals a new detail with each perusal. Much like the nuances of the music contained on the album itself. (As an experiment, put a mirror down the centre of the cover artwork. The results are equally fascinating and terrifying. It encapsulates perfectly the idea of Michael and dichotomy. Try it.)

Certainly, the promotional campaign for the *Dangerous* album did little to disassociate Michael from the Occult, what with David Lynch – fresh from the supernatural horror TV Series *Twin Peaks* – hired to direct the *Dangerous* teaser: a surrealist nightmare set to the loudening sound of industrial drums, in which Michael's head emerges from a fiery pit, before steadily floating towards the viewer across a barren, hellish landscape and finally settling on a close-up of Michael's eyes.

Furthermore, immediately prior to Michael's appearance on the stage during the *Dangerous* tour, Carl Orff's connotation-laden classic 'O Fortuna' - instantly recognisable as the music announcing someone's imminent doom in horror-movie, *The Omen* – was played as the soundtrack to the accompanying idol-worship video, *Brace Yourself*. Michael also used a sample from another horror-flick inspired soundtrack in 'Human Nature' – namely, 'Tubular Bells'. As used with chilling effect in *The Exorcist*.

Along with the love of their mother, of music, of animals, of other children, of cartoons and of theme parks, the supernatural also factors on the rather limited list of interests entertained by the ten-year old boy – as does an acute sense of injustice, and an innate need to rectify it. Whatever dabbling with the supernatural Michael may have done, it carries with it this air of naivety.

Besides, in counterbalance, for every 'Scream' there was a 'Smile' (indeed, the *HIStory* album itself can be interpreted as a journey of catharsis); for every angry spit there was an ethereal melody (sometimes in the very same song – 'HIStory' and 'Morphine', to name but two. Michael even used the flute from John Williams' *Jaws* theme in 'Heal The World'); for every demonic entrance, there was an angel's embrace. In *This Is It*, the only examples of music from the *Invincible* album that we hear, are the gentle 'Speechless' and its macabre sonic antithesis, 'Threatened'.

When 'Scream' was released, critical commentators queried how the ordinary person could relate to the song, considering the uniqueness of the subject matter that had spurred its inception. The response was that the refrain, "Stop pressurin' me" could be interpreted and extrapolated by listeners, who would make it relevant to the general frustrations of everyday life. The same principle applies to what was the Double A-side track to 'Scream': 'Childhood' - which can be individually appreciated by anyone that feels the need to implore others to attempt to understand them by asking them to see the injustices they suffered as youths. As Michael sang,

"Before you judge me try hard to love me / Look within your heart, then ask / Have you seen my childhood?"

In the same way that one need not necessarily have been the biggest star on the planet in order to experience instances of pressure, one neither had to have been the biggest star on the planet to have suffered a stolen childhood. The Double A-side singles of 'Scream' and 'Childhood' were two sides of the same coin.

***

Michael liked to draw attention by using contrasting sounds in his work: on the *Victory* album the ballad 'Be Not Always' was followed by the funk-rock track 'State Of Shock'; on *Bad*, 'Speed Demon' was followed by 'Liberian Girl'; on *Dangerous*, 'Heal The World' followed 'Can't Let Her Get Away'; on *HIStory*, 'Tabloid Junkie' followed 'Childhood'; on *Invincible*, 'Speechless' was followed by '2000 Watts'. In live performances, 'She's Out Of My Life' was followed by 'I Want You Back'. As a technique for pricking the ears, it was certainly effective. Michael also used the approach within stand-alone songs. During live performances, too - in 'Working Day and Night', for example, Michael thought nothing of following a white rock female guitar solo with a spurt of slap-bass. Indeed, subtle segues are found few and far between in Michael's work, though when they are, they are devastating. Suddenly discovering oneself somehow immersed in the unbridled joy of 'Rock With You' after its transition from the anguish of 'I'll Be There' on the *Bad* tour is an experience of absolute beauty.

Michael embodied balance. It was an intrinsic feature of his dance: pointing in one direction whilst thrusting his hip to the other side, before repeating the move the other way; grabbing his crotch whilst simultaneously incorporating the sign of the cross; walking forwards and backwards at the same time; and – the very embodiment of the philosophy – the toe-stand.

***

There are those that criticise some of the tactics Michael deployed in his efforts to promote his idea of the healing power of love. However, Michael had the talent and work ethic to back up his propaganda machine. All the promotion in the world will only get you so far without the requisite talent and industry. Besides, what's wrong with the use of any technique, when the message being promulgated is to love one another? As far as role models go, there is none better.

Throughout the eighties, Michael was that rare public figure: encouraged to be liked by parents, with this encouragement enthusiastically reciprocated by their children. He was a true unifier. It's hardly surprising a world governed by greed and funded by hate chose to bring him down. But in doing so, they martyred him.

Michael's success was down to his mastery of all the components of being a superstar: he combined his otherworldly talent with his transient physicality as a means to an end, to remain relevant-yet-enigmatic in an effort to further his fame, and hence his message. In spite of all the change, there was an immutable undercurrent that ran through all his conduits of conveyance - that an appreciation of the wisdom of children is the essence of, and answer to, world peace.

CHAPTER THREE

Show me a hero and I will write you a tragedy.

F. SCOTT FITZGERALD

In order to get close enough to the microphone when recording songs, the child Michael stood atop an apple box. From this elevated position, he conveyed a supernaturally precocious ability for perfectly expressing the joy of romantic love.

The paradox of Michael's back-catalogue is that the themes present in his childhood material (having been written by adults) were mature beyond his years, whilst the ideas he explored in his self-penned adult work were more akin to those that would inspire a child.

As a child, Michael could merely imagine what romantic love was like, yet he managed to relay its emotions with a visceral conviction. His song 'With a Child's Heart' is advice on attempting to assuage the tumultuousness of life by approaching each day with the carefree attitude of youth. Contrasted with the other songs of his childhood career, in which he effortlessly relays the euphoria of adult love, the song 'With a Child's Heart' anomalously drips with the tangible pain of a subconscious awareness of the irony in the words he is singing. As Michael said during an interview in 1980,

"When I was small I didn't really know what I was doing, I just sang and it just came out sounding… pretty good."

The formative *Jackson 5* years left no-one in doubt with regards Michael's capacity for conveying emotion through his voice. Though it was not until Michael left Motown, that we were requited with this voice singing songs that he had authored himself. With 'Blues Away' came the epiphany - many artists never write a song as important as this in their entire career. Yet, this track - from the eponymous *The Jacksons* album - their first after unshackling themselves of the artistic constraints that bound them at Motown - was a mere taster; a tantalising teaser of what was to come.

Whereupon one need look no further than *Destiny* - the subsequent *Epic* release from *The Jacksons*.

The opening track - the bassline bonanza that is 'Blame It on the Boogie' - is the sole song on the record not written by the brothers (though, coincidentally, it was penned by a Michael Jackson namesake). The album palpably throbs with both joy and heartbreak. The autobiographical nature of the lyrical themes are prescient of the standard ideas we would come to recognise in Michael's solo work, referencing as they do: insecurity and success as bedfellows; the escapism of dance; and the loneliness of being misunderstood.

Concerning the latter theme, the song 'Bless His Soul' is perhaps the most touching: not merely in the context of the *Destiny* album, but also when considering Michael's canon of work as a whole. The bridge contains the refrain, "The life you're leading is dangerous," with the melody in that final word 'dangerous' reminiscent of the chorus of the title track that Michael would record thirteen years later. What with the theme of 'Bless His Soul' addressing how, "You gotta start doing what's right for you / 'Cos life is being happy yourself" - and how when not living by this philosophy, life becomes "dangerous", the mirroring becomes poignantly prophetic. Of course, when Michael eventually did begin living how he desired, his life became very dangerous indeed.

The Jacksons' ensuing release after *Destiny* was the album *Triumph*. The short film for the opening track features this Michael-penned voiceover:

"In the beginning, the land was pure – even in the early morning light, you could see the beauty in the forms of nature. Soon, men and women of every colour and shape would be here too – and they would find it all-too easy not to see the colours, and to ignore the beauty in each other. But they would never lose sight of the dream of a better world that they could build together – in triumph."

It is spoken as the camera pans across a gorgeous vista of daybreak over a deserted landscape. The conclusion of the voiceover is the signal for the horns to ignite the iconic rhythm of *The Jacksons* classic, 'Can You Feel It'.

In spite of the short film's inclusion in a 2001 poll listing the *100 Greatest Music Videos*, the spectacle that is the 'Can You Feel It' promo is nowadays often overlooked. However, in 1981 - the year of its release - the short film's state-of-the-art visual effects popped the eyes and dropped the jaws of anyone that saw it, as demonstrated quite clearly by the host's gasp of disbelief when introducing its premiere on *American Bandstand*. Prior to 'Can You Feel It', the accepted format of music videos had been that of a band in a studio, pretending to sing and perform their instruments in front of a static camera. The conception and execution of the 'Can You Feel It' project was nothing short of revolutionary. It was a vanguard; it was the work of a visionary.

(The *MTV Michael Jackson Video Vanguard Award* was named after Michael in 1991, in honour of the culture-altering contribution that was his dedication to promoting the music video as a credible artistic medium. Still, between the years of 1993 and 2005, the award was only intermittently presented. 1997 was one of the years in which it was – when Mark Romanek was granted the prize, after having directed the short film, 'Scream'. However, since 2005, when Michael was cleared of the child molestation allegations, the eponymous award has been a frequent feature of the *MTV Video Music Awards* show. MTV would do well to remember that they would not even exist if it were not for Michael.)

Upon leaving Motown, *The Jacksons* created their own production company – *Peacock Productions*. They explained their choice of name for this venture by saying,

"Through the ages, the peacock has been honoured and praised for its attractive, illustrious beauty. Of all the bird family, the peacock is the only bird that integrates all colours into one, and displays this radiance of fire only when in love. We, like the peacock, try to integrate all races into one through the love of music."

The peacock feather is utilised in the 'Can You Feel It' video, as an emblem of hope that descends upon humanity, after the light of the sun is extinguished by an eclipse. The anti-racism theme is encapsulated by the lyric, "Because the blood inside of me / Is inside of you". It is a reminder that regardless of our race, in sufferance we all cry the same coloured tears.

In 1980, Michael mused,

"You go to our concerts and you see every race out there – waving hands, and they're holding hands, and they're smiling, and they're dancing – all colours. That's what's great. That's what will keep me going."

The significance of a group of black men - products of the decade that brought an end to racial segregation in the United States - wielding their substantial influence cannot be understated. Their message was to encourage progression – that, in spite of their forefathers having suffered the torture and inhumanity of slavery, any ambitions of world peace involve every one of us moving forward, celebratory of our differences, but united. Accusations were levelled at *The Jacksons* that the video was a mass Jehovah's Witness promotion and recruitment attempt. And that's cynicism for you. Nonetheless, a connection does indeed exist between Christianity and peacocks: in the religion's early incarnation, the peacock was utilised as a totem for immortality. This was due to the fact that after a peacock died, its feathers remained fresh and vibrant, in spite of the decaying flesh they covered.

One of the jackets that Michael wore to perform 'Jam' on the *Dangerous* tour (the artwork on the associated album also incorporating an image of a peacock) - a song in which Michael took to the stage to strut and state - is reminiscent of the shimmer and sheen of the peacock's feather. At first glance, both the jacket and the feather are made up of what are ostensibly solid colours; but with closer inspection, it is revealed that they are actually comprised of myriad, minutely varied colourations that integrate to appear as one. A comparable analogy can be used for the many layers that combine to create a song – such as the way the bassline from 'I Want You Back' emphasises the harmonies whilst complimenting the melody. As such, the peacock feather provides us with a perfect metaphor for the political and philosophical leanings of Michael. It is one that suggests that the growing individualistic nature of the people of the world - Michael himself taking individualism to its ultimate conclusion - in which the shackles of patriarchy are being dismantled, need not necessarily be an ominous thing. So long as the onus is on using one's gifts and talents for the potentiation of the happiness of others.

***

Michael had mastered the soulful evocation of romantic love by the time he was a teenager. It's no wonder he evolved to write love letters to planet Earth. Saying that, people often misconstrue that Michael's mission to heal the world was a latter-day attitude that he adopted – a moral obligation he undertook as a result of the fame he achieved due to *Thriller* – but the truth is, that way back in the *Jackson 5*, Michael was already singing such lyrics as "We can stand, despite all of the dark lies / And we can build a world that is right / We can be the children of the light".

Then, in the seventies, as soon as Michael was granted the opportunity to record his self-penned music, he wrote lyrics such as "All the children of the world should be / Loving each other wholeheartedly." The idea of the use of childhood innocence to redeem humanity had been entwined in his soul at an early age.

There is an absurd conspiracy theory promulgated by some that denies Michael the talent of songwriting. He remarked on this odd perspective,

"People used to underestimate my ability as a songwriter. They didn't think of me as a songwriter, so when I started coming up with songs, they'd look at me like: "Who really wrote that?" I don't know what they must have thought - that I had someone back in the garage who was writing them for me? But time cleared up those misconceptions. You always have to prove yourself to people and so many of them don't want to believe."

Michael was a man who had grown up in recording studios; recording studios in which he was the protégé of the genius songwriter Stevie Wonder. Why wouldn't he be able to write songs? Indeed, perhaps his most prolific songwriting phase was during the period he duetted with Stevie Wonder, on the tracks 'Get It' and 'Just Good Friends' – though it is somewhat ironic that 'Just Good Friends' was one of only two tracks on the *Bad* album that Michael didn't write. Michael's creative fertility at this stage was further demonstrated on the *Bad 25* bonus disc, which featured a collection of *Bad* era demos evidencing nothing short of an embarrassment of unreleased riches. (Though most eventually did see the authorised light of day as finished tracks in one way or another – 'Free' becoming 'Elizabeth I Love You', 'Al Capone' evolving into 'Smooth Criminal' and 'Price Of Fame' reminiscent of 'Who Is It'. The chord sequence in 'Abortion Papers' ultimately evolved into 'Jam'. Now there's a sentence.)

Michael's songwriting process is sometimes dismissed as being vague, what with his perpetual referral to the music 'coming from God' or the 'Giving Tree' – and in his insistence that he was naught but a vessel. However, in ancient Greece and ancient Rome, the contemporaneous accepted belief system was that creativity is the effects of celestial spirits expressing an awareness of their existence through human acts of artistry: that a genius was a divine entity abiding in the walls of an artisan's house, invisibly assisting the corporeal creator. In Plato's *Realm of the Forms*, the philosopher muses that the ideal form of everything already exists, with everything on Earth being only an inferior copy. For example, there does exist a perfect circle in the world of the forms, but there can never be one on Earth. Plato dismissed art as unnecessarily distracting from the forms – that art is an imitation of a copy, and that any good art would have to come from knowledge of the forms; whereupon - such as in the case of Michael - it could manifest through a terrestrial recipient as an uninterrupted divine stream. The earthbound creator merely being - to borrow Jermaine Jackson's take on Conrad Murray's responsibility for the death of Michael – "the finger to a bigger hand."

The childlike quality of Michael's artistry is precisely what makes it so estimable; the capacity to successfully express emotion and ideas so succinctly is the exclusive domain of the artistic greats. Paul McCartney mentioned to Michael that he should modify the lyrics to 'The Girl Is Mine', as he thought they were too naïve. Michael responded that he was more concerned with "the feel" of the piece. Michael's utilisation of childlike qualities in his music is exemplified in such songs as 'Wanna Be Startin' Somethin'' and 'They Don't Care About Us' – the choruses of both being reminiscent of playground chants. The "feel" Michael referred to in conversation with McCartney is very evident in these tracks, though neither the theme nor the lyrics to these examples could ever be construed as "naïve."

When Michael spoke of his work being inspired by children, it was perhaps in a more direct way than people interpreted.

Michael's refusal to take credit for the rhythms and melodies that inspired and entertained a planet – consistently attributing the results to a force beyond himself - is a beautiful depiction of Michael's level of humility.

There is a demo version of 'Beat It' that simultaneously showcases Michael's creative process and inherently modest nature. The track begins with a mumbled introduction, in which Michael stumbles over his words with a humble hesitance. He then proceeds to immaculately vocalise every instrument and sonic nuance that he wants the musicians to reproduce in the studio with their instruments. It is mind-blowing.

There is a further example that demonstrates how Michael managed to retain this admirable trait of humility even after a life lauded with plaudits and insidious sycophancy. It is exhibited in the 'Billie Jean' rehearsal featured in *This Is It*. As Michael performs, his molten dance moves etch expressions of pure astonishment onto the faces of the small crowd watching him. At the conclusion to the spectacle, Michael shyly bats off the resultant standing ovation with the embarrassed words, "Ah… at least we get a feel for it."

Michael naturally took his awareness of the presence of the divine during moments of creativity into the recording studio with him. During the recording process, Co-Executive Producer Quincy Jones held dear the philosophy, "always leave some space to let God walk through the room." (Incidentally, some suggest that Michael's early solo success was purely down to the input of Quincy. However, Quincy had been reluctant to include 'Smooth Criminal' on the *Bad* album - a track that would become one of the most iconic of Michael's career.)

There is an audio clip in existence that was recorded during the genesis of 'Give in to Me', in which Michael is heard suggesting that the session guitarist should just jam, as that's where ideas come from, "It would be neat for you sometime to just hook up your electric guitar… and just start playing, and get me a mic' and… out of the moment… a lot of magic is created out of the moment like that… it really is."

The musician Prince is renowned for his jam sessions and for his belief in their capacity to create - something that burdened Michael with a sincere concern. Michael worried that, if he fell asleep, the genie would bypass him. As he divulged in conversation with longterm artistic collaborator Kenny Ortega, "You don't understand – if I'm not there to receive these ideas, God might give them to Prince."

On the face of it, this seems an almost comical and stereotypically 'Michael-esque' concern to possess. Yet, he is by no means the sole artist to have been discomfited by such worries. The American poet Ruth Stone regaled a story of how - when growing up and working in the fields of rural Virginia - she would often sense a poem suddenly approaching her from the horizon, whereupon she would have to physically race the poem back to the house before it could hit her without her having the means to write it down. Sometimes she would lose the contest - at which point, the poem would continue on its enigmatic voyage through the ether, and she would have to reluctantly concede that the work was meant "for another poet".

Of course, the success to which any artist interprets their perceived divinations from the celestial is entirely subjective. But it's interesting to ponder what Michael would have done with Prince's 'Purple Rain'; or, indeed - what Prince would have done with 'Earth Song'. Prince has had many attempts at world-redemption songs, though these have always been expressed through the thinly veiled guise of the Jehovah's Witness solution. Michael also – unsurprisingly - utilised the Jehovah's Witness approach (especially as a member of *The Jacksons*), but seemed more capable of employing Biblical passages without sounding like he had just knocked on your door with a copy of *The Watchtower* in hand.

The origin of the expression "with great power comes great responsibility" is unknown, though both prime candidates of Stan Lee and Franklin D. Roosevelt were heroes of Michael's. Its essence is synonymous with Christ's words, "To whom much has been given, much will be expected", which again, is something Michael would have been very familiar with due to his upbringing. And what did Michael choose to use his great power for? To spread an ethos of love.

Michael had far greater commercial success with his 'redeemer records' than Prince did, and perhaps there exists some correlation between these relative successes and the respective echelons of fame achieved by the two artists. Michael shall forevermore inhabit a more prestigious plane of fame than Prince does (the litmus test for this being the showing of a photograph of someone famous to the inhabitants of a remote African village, then seeing if they are familiar with the person in said picture. Not only is Michael recognised where Prince is not, but Michael was actually crowned King of the Sanwi in the west African village of Krinjabo – whose people observed two days of mourning upon receiving the news of his death).

Further examples of Michael's level of fame are evidenced in such accolades as the *Thriller* album being chosen as the only music video preserved in the United States Library of Congress; that he featured in *Smithsonian* magazine's list of the '100 Most Significant Americans of All Time'; and that the *British Council* regarded 'The influence of the life and music of the American singer Michael Jackson, 1958-2009' as one of the 80 most significant cultural events in the history of the world.

At school, we used to play a game in which the question posed was whether one would rather be rich or famous. I can't remember which way I swayed, but I'd say it's a good bet Michael would have chosen fame, whereas Prince would have chosen wealth. This is not to infer that either of these options were the artists' primary motivation for success - for both of them, the freedom of artistic expression was paramount, as evidenced by the pair protesting about their treatment at the hands of their respective record companies. Regardless, all great art – which the two men indubitably created - comes first and foremost from a house of honesty.

In contrast to Michael's back catalogue being instantly available to access and enjoy on YouTube (bar any uploaded voice comparison tests of the Cascio tracks, incidentally – they're taken down in minutes), Prince is notoriously precious over copyright infringement, employing an army of legal staff to trawl the Internet and wave cease-and-desist demands at anyone construed to be crossing the copyright line.

In Michael's song, 'Price of Fame', he lets us know that his father made him fully aware of the dangers correlative to the altitude of fame that Michael was shooting for. The risks were nonetheless confronted by Michael. As he sang in 'Dirty Diana',

"I'll be the freak you can taunt /And I don't care what you say / I want to go too far / I'll be your everything / If you make me a star".

These risks ultimately becoming manifest through the infamy that arrived with the molestation allegations. With the tragic irony being Michael's pursuit of fame being driven by a desire to spread his message of love as a healing force for the disadvantaged children of the world; whilst the architects of his fall from grace were motivated by money. The consequence of this tragedy was that the vacuum created by the potency of Michael's drug of fame became inversely correlated with his self-defeating reliance on analgesics.

Of course, Michael's penchant for a Salvation Army bargain and his lyrical complaints in songs such as 'Leave Me Alone', in which he sings, "Time after time I gave you all of my money" contradict the idea of his being apathetic towards financial success - although the bone of contention that inspired the 'Leave Me Alone' lyric appears to be borne more of a sense of being wrongly done by, rather than a reluctance to help. In the Glenda Jackson tapes - in which Michael is recorded without his knowledge - Michael bemoans the regular requests for money asked of him by his father. In this particular instance, half a billion dollars.

Yet, Michael's willingness to stump up the surplus cash required to finance his short films - the most expensive of all time - provide a more concrete idea of Michael's frame of mind in the quandary between money and fame. Too, was his complete lack of hesitation in profligacy when it came to hiring recording studios (though the sumptuousness of the sonics contained in the music produced - compared to that of Prince's - speaks for itself). And let's not forget Michael's fondness for booking out multiple floors of hotel rooms whilst on tour (though the opportunity of having all that space in which to ride around in golf carts might account for this particular fiscal idiosyncrasy).

Michael's relationship with money was certainly a complex one. In his song 'Money' he condemns greed with all the venom of - to quote Prince - "snakes of every colour, nationality and size". And the parlance with which he rattles off the list of money moguls, "Vanderbilt, Morgan, Trump, Rockefeller, Carnegie, Getty... Getty... Getty, Getty, Getty, Getty" is nothing short of sinister. There is even a version of the song 'Money' in which Michael calls out press emperor Rupert Murdoch: a man often with the balance of power in swaying the opinion of the populous of entire countries - be that who should win *X-Factor*, who should rule a country, or whether or not a country should engage in war.

Michael was not a man to shy away from controversial socio-political matters. On the contrary, he considered it his duty, what with his being the most famous man in the world. As he stated at the *Bollywood Awards* in 2000,

"I've always believed that the real measure of celebrity success was not just how famous he becomes, but what he does with that fame and fortune".

In an interview with UK television immediately prior to the first 1988 Wembley *Bad* concert, Michael's then-manager Frank Dileo revealed that Michael said whatever he needed to say on the stage. Similarly, when his mother implored him to respond to tabloid criticism and conjecture, Michael simply responded that he communicated through his music – an ethos that would eventually bear the strange fruit that is the *HIStory* album.

Michael was lambasted for the repetitiveness of his themes (in itself supportive of the idea that Michael did indeed write his own songs). But - just as any other artist - he was simply inspired by what he knew, and what he was going through.

Michael said, "Music is the soundtrack to life. It plays the melody of our being." Therefore, hand-in-hand with the change in tune that was his treatment by the press, so did his muses mutate: from artistry inspired by the sweet naivety of nature, to craft generated by the infernal rage of injustice. As Michael explained,

"The more you hit something hard, the more hardened it becomes - the stronger it becomes. And that's what's happened."

This metamorphosis is illustrated rather poignantly by contrasting the carefree lyrics from the Temperton-penned 'Off The Wall' title-track, in which Michael joyously croons, "Gotta leave that nine-to-five upon the shelf / And just enjoy yourself" with the comparable lyrics from *Invincible* outtake, 'Shout' - in which he sings, "Eating each other alive just to survive the nine-to-five / Every single day is trouble while we struggle and strive".

(Incidentally, the caustic, industrial-funk, political-polemic track 'Shout' was only cut from *Invincible* at the eleventh hour, in order to make room for the heartfelt ballad, 'You Are My Life'. Only Michael could make two such polar-opposite tunes interchangeable on an album.)

***

After the unprecedented successes of *Thriller* and *Bad*, Michael understood absolutely that his follow-up would be a globally significant record. But he took the risk of changing direction and parting ways with Quincy Jones, becoming Executive Producer himself, and creating an experimental masterpiece that demonstrated his omnipotence over several different musical genres.

The relative subtlety involved in the rock-funk fusion that was 'Beat It' was flagrantly discarded: the *Dangerous* album campaign kicked off with the explicit genre-amalgam hit, 'Black or White' - a shameless attempt at unifying different cultures through song, using a mash-up of musical styles. You can call it a cynical ploy to appeal to a wider range of buyers, or you can call it a man using his leverage to bring about something positive, but I would say one need look no further than 'Heal The World' for the truth.

Michael produced the entirety of 'Heal The World' with the sole purpose of doing what he could to make the world a better place. The track is an incongruous curiosity on the *Dangerous* album - a jarring shift that marks the transition from the New Jack Swing first half of the record, to the 'pot pourri' (to borrow Michael's expression) of genres that make up the second. It certainly wasn't a song included to appease the critics. Its incorporation left him wide-open to ridicule. Ergo, it seems intellectually disingenuous to then claim it as part of a cynical ploy for sales. 'Heal The World' is a pacifier for the planet, sneaked past the Sony suits onto what was primarily - at the time - a trendy New Jack Swing record. 'Heal The World' is placed precisely where it is in order to be noticed. To make a point. Which other artist would, or could, do that?

In a similar vein, there's also a further reason why 'Come Together' was oddly included on the *HIStory* album – situated directly after the song, 'Money'. *The Beatles* track symbolised his acquisition of the band's music catalogue. The quality and magnitude of Michael's art has ensured it an infinite longevity, but the ingenious subtleties of it are often overlooked.

On the *Dangerous* track, 'Why You Wanna Trip On Me' - although not written by him - Michael waxes lyrical on the state of the world and the relative insignificance of his personal life, even inferring at one stage that AIDS is a man-made virus (although the way he expresses the interjection "ha" after singing about "strange diseases" begs the question as whether this is also a dual reference to Michael's, at-the-time-unannounced, vitiligo).

The term 'Punk' is perhaps not the first adjective that springs to mind when it comes to describing Michael ('Goth' maybe – considering his predilection for the macabre). Yet, if we apply the prerequisites used to identify punk behaviour, in the true spirit of the term - a stubborn refusal to bow down to orthodoxy and authority - it could be argued that Michael suddenly becomes punk's paragon.

The propensity for analysis in Michael's songwriting is indefatigable. And Michael's songwriting genius wasn't limited to any particular heyday, either: the latterday track 'We've Had Enough', for example, containing the lyric, "What did these soldiers come here for? / If they're for peace - why is there war?"

Michael was a martyr for innocence. He died engulfed by an inherent sadness that he could not realise his idealistic perception of the world; a romantic perception borne of a lifetime of being a sounding board for love. And, as the human being who'd experienced being loved more than anyone else in existence, who was better qualified to state that love is the answer? The song 'Heal the World' has its detractors, but who can deny the sincerity with which it is sung? That song is all the proof required to know who Michael was. Michael felt the pain of people's suffering. We saw Michael as myriad characters, but they were always beneath the umbrella of him as humanitarian; a record-breaking philanthropist. He conveyed his beautiful ideal to anyone that would listen: that the innocence of childhood has an untouchable preciousness, and should be universally treated with unimpeachable honour. This is what Michael represents.

***

Michael described being on stage thusly,

"You are connected to a higher source… you just go with the moment and you become one with the spirit, and not to sound religious… but it is very spiritual, very much like religion… it's a God-given gift… I'm honoured to have been given it… it's fun to become one with the audience, it's a oneness."

It's this repeated experience of "oneness" with so many people – a recurrent experience Michael had to a unique degree - that I believe drove Michael's political leanings.

In the crowd-immersing short film that cranks up the anticipation prior to Michael's explosive entrance onto the *HIStory* tour stage, the audience is taken on a ride through historic global events. Michael's music and iconography is interspersed with video of the moon landings; images of Mother Teresa; and speeches from Martin Luther King Junior: events and people appropriate to the majesty of Michael and his achievements. The rollercoaster then takes us into the Sistine

Chapel, which we float through in seraphim silence, taking time to admire the exquisite pulchritude of the surrounding art – before being plunged into a dark-but-fiery nightmare, a depiction of bleak emptiness inspired by God-knows-what. Then, before gracing and scintillating a stadium for the umpteenth time – to entertain yet another hundred-thousand people piqued to see him – Michael makes a quick detour to go and sort out that minor irritation: war.

The *HIStory* tour is much-maligned. The audacity with which Michael utilised lip-syncing was lambasted by many critics at the time. Lung damage was described in his autopsy. It had been a longstanding issue – likely a symptom of his being a victim of lupus. Michael, being a very private man, tried to keep his medical problems a secret (sometimes to the detriment of his public relations – Michael had been becoming noticeably paler for years before he revealed his vitiligo), but the breathing problems became evermore evidenced by the fact that his reliance on playback increased with subsequent tours. With hindsight, it stands to reason that this was due to his lung damage being a degenerative condition exacerbated by being a professional singer.

It is unfortunate that the *HIStory* tour ushered in an age of pop star lip-syncing (after all, if the King of Pop can do it, surely anyone can? But then – Michael was forever the trendsetter), as there now exists a frightening ubiquity of post-*Disney* puppets that flagrantly employ auto-tune and playback with the cynical sole intent of selling capitalist standards of sexual imagery to children. At least when Michael's illness forced him to lip-sync, he was selling a message of peace and goodwill. (And dancing a fair bit, too - a very special spectacle, itself worth the entrance fee). All of this being done whilst suffering with various extreme physical pains, acquired as a result of dedicating his life to entertaining and educating us through song and dance.

The fact that Michael toured at all is testament to his work ethic and dedication to his message. The reason Michael grew tired of touring was because of the Sword of Damocles that was the inevitable drug dependency that would resume in order to get through a gruelling two-year global schedule. With regards the intermittent screaming he began to utilise – it may well have been the subconscious, spontaneous vocal expression of a frustrated human being, universally renowned for his unique voice, having to contend with age-and-illness-related vocal deterioration. Let's not forget that Michael had been touring the world and singing professionally for thirty years by this point. Or perhaps the reason for the screaming has a simpler solution. After all - why do people scream? To draw attention to their plight. The *HIStory* tour was the twilight of Michael's career. And ultimately, attempting to live up to the unrealistic and selfish demands of an ungrateful public, *This Is It* - becoming the midnight of his career – concluded with his death.

The rare examples of Michael singing live in the latter years ('Smile' and 'The Lost Children' seen in candid footage and 'I Just Can't Stop Loving You', 'Don't Stop Til You Get Enough', Speechless' and 'Human Nature' during *This Is It*) are just snippets – Michael could not sustain a vocal performance for any length of time. He certainly didn't possess the physical capability to complete a fifty-night run at the *O2*. The Brunei Royal Concert gig of 1996 – just prior to the *HIStory* tour– was the last time Michael sang the majority of a show live. But this was a standalone performance, not part of a tour. The 3D gimmickry, pyrotechnics and the like, that became increasingly prevalent, were all distractions from the fact that Michael as a live vocal performer was becoming a spent force. But he still endeavoured to give his fans a good show. As Katharine Hepburn observes in *The Legend Continues* documentary, "I think what makes him a star is - he can do it, and you can't help looking at him."

And, sure enough, the *HIStory* tour as a dance showcase and vehicle for Michael's humanitarian efforts, was indeed spectacular. As the stage got bigger and bigger, it gave Michael the necessary increased space to bring his vision of philanthropic theatre to life – an untouchable catalogue of unique and iconic choreography. However, the expanding stage also made Michael look more and more alone up there. This being the only shame in the *HIStory* tour. Anyway, show me a contemporary lip-syncing artist that can deliver a show even half as good. You can't.

In the documentary *Michael Jackson's Private Home Movies*, there is a much-loved segment in which Michael protests an interviewer who is determined to put a positive spin on a conversation about going on tour. Michael exclaims, "I go through hell touring!" After some persuading from the persistent interviewer, Michael sarcastically claims, "I love to tour!" It was Jermaine Jackson that spoke of Michael's apprehension before tours; an anxiety stirred by the known inevitability of his having to resort to medication to fulfil its obligations. The artificial stimulation of artists to meet such demands is a practice as old as the industry: Judy Garland was fed amphetamines to 'help' her keep to *The Wizard of Oz* filming schedule.

Saying all this, it is quite evident that Michael is happy during periods of the *HIStory* tour - more so than he appears on the *Dangerous* tour. He can be seen smiling as he performs, no doubt enjoying the knowledge of his career being back on track, a fact made evident by an appreciative and admiring crowd of up to one-hundred-thousand people, gratefully enraptured in their opportunity to see a legendary, historically-significant figure renowned for his dancing genius. Who is dancing. And all for £17.50.

***

One particular set-piece of the *HIStory* tour that critics disdainfully discuss, is the flamboyant theatrics of the show's version of 'Earth

Song'. At the conclusion to the performance, Michael stands – Tiananmen Square-style - in front of an encroaching tank, before facing off the disembarked soldier, removing his gun, and replacing it with a sunflower: a gesture clearly referencing the iconic photograph of Jan Rose Kasmir at an anti-Vietnam war rally at the Pentagon, in 1967. What people forget, is that Michael – with his being a uniquely global figure - had to communicate his message without having to rely on spoken language. Something he did through creating dramatic, easily-interpreted visual statements. Michael wasn't about to let the slight inconvenience of 6,500 extant languages become an obstacle in his mission for peace. The 'Earth Song' performance is the 'Heal The World' lyric, "turn their swords into ploughshares" made manifest. This Biblical concept formed part of the practical solution in the fulfilment of Michael's dream: a common-sense notion as old as time, yet perpetually dismissed by greedy and fearful governments across the globe.

'Earth Song' in itself isn't exactly devoid of ingenious musical and linguistic nuances - what with the chorus itself being a plaintive cry for the plight of the planet and her "weeping shores". As well as its unmistakable melody, of course. Michael always said that melody is king, that melodies remain eternally unique, and are what people will still whistle in a hundred years' time, regardless of progressions in technology and future production techniques. Melody knows no language barrier.

We all have our favourite Michael hiccups, "hoos", grunts and yelps: the inimitable minutiae of Michael's work. His adlibs - often imploring over a soaring, climactic crescendo - were executed like no-one else could. Michael always signed his best work with a particularly sumptuous "hee hee". Though the "hee hee" was no mere gimmick: it being more a watermark than a trademark. Some of his most 'wholesome' "hee hees" are found on self-penned songs, with 'They Don't Care About Us' containing a prime example. Again, "hee hee" was a universally recognised sound.

(Another indicator of Michael's pride in his self-penned pieces was in their inclusion in concert set-lists. 'Working Day And Night' and 'Heartbreak Hotel', particularly. But on the *HIStory* tour, Michael even dropped 'Man In The Mirror' for 'HIStory', and 'Human Nature' – having previously been a set-list certainty – was replaced with 'Stranger In Moscow'.)

The *HIStory* tour contains – by far – the most instances of Michael playfully interacting with the crowd. There are many enjoyable moments - one particularly noteworthy example being the drama-stoking Charlie Chaplin tribute that precedes the iconic drums of 'Billie Jean'. The extent of the lip-syncing lends to this playfulness (perhaps epitomised during 'Blood On The Dance Floor', in which, at one point – in-between shoulder-snapping his way across the stage – Michael literally lies down on the floor). Too, the prevalence of lip-syncing paradoxically means that there is much joy in discovering a spontaneous yelp or hiccup caught by the microphone. Comedians learn their routines down to the minutiae of an equivalent comedic beat. As the most experienced entertainer on Earth, Michael understood that a framework to operate around was vital for successful delivery, with his ability to improvise choreography akin to that of a jazz veteran.

Concerning the comedian analogy, it's relevant to note Michael's love for slapstick humour. He was a huge fan of *The Stooges*, even writing the foreword to a biography on them,

"*The Stooges*' craziness helped me to relax and to escape life's burdens. They influenced me so much that I even wrote a song about them… Curly was definitely my favourite Stooge. He was unquestionably a comic genius who understood ad-libbing better than anyone… underneath the smile may have been a tear - after all, he was a clown. But it is our duty as entertainers to satisfy the people - to give of our souls even if it hurts."

Michael rarely riffed randomly, but when he did, in the context of the *HIStory* tour, they are moments cherished by fans. It's the very reason why treasured compilations of these moments exist as videos on YouTube. They are the equivalent to an inside joke. And all the more entertaining for it.

Seeing the occasions in which Michael instructs the sound engineers whilst performing – often seamlessly, via a dissatisfied raise of the eyes towards the back of the stage, or through a gesture incorporated into a dance move that is requesting an increase in volume levels - are priceless. Then there are the more overt examples, such as towards the end of 'I Just Can't Stop Loving You' during the Brunei Royal Concert, in which Michael turns to the rear of the stage and in a good-natured tone, enquiringly sings, "Brad, what you gonna do?" The enthusiastic live vocalisations prior to the first verse of 'Jam' at the beginning of the same gig also suggest that Michael was in a positive mood about being back in front of an audience.

Also in Brunei, there is an almost self-parodying instance of Michael forgetting the lyrics to 'Beat It' and replacing them with any syllables that fit the rhythm - at least it gives us a great example of what Rod Temperton meant regarding using staccato rhythms when writing for Michael - and it's certainly better than one example from a *HIStory* tour concert, in which Michael is seen forgetting the lip-synced lyrics to 'Beat It' as he puts his face into the camera - before putting his hand over his mouth to disguise the fact.

In much the same way that Michael could inhabit the necessary emotion to so convincingly convey what he wanted to express in his songs – an innate trait evident in him since being eleven and singing 'I'll Be There' – he somehow manages to also do whilst lip-syncing. And when he lip-synced in the *Jackson 5*– who berated him then? I'm sure Michael sincerely wished he could have sung live in the latter years, but it was beyond his – or anyone's – physical capacity. Lungs damaged after singing since the age of eleven in smoky venues, or not.

***

Though Michael effused a childlike innocence, as with all superheroes, there existed the alter ego: the self-mutilated manifestation of a tragically mistaken anger with himself for perennially failing to compete with the paradigm of perfectionism demanded from him during his youth. Michael was an anarchic utopian: he was like a river - when peaceable, you could sit by him, close your eyes, relax and be bewitched by his chortling ruminations; yet, when you encountered the spontaneous rage of his waterfall, you heard his white noise, his turbid despair. Both occur in his music: a spectrum of sadness; a many-colour melancholy of melodies that range from the placid to the brutal. Both are enigmatic. Both are beautiful. Both are never more prominent than in the song 'Morphine'.

In 'Morphine', Michael gently delivers the words "Demerol, Demerol, oh God he's taking Demerol" whilst the mechanical bleeps and beeps of medical equipment are played in the background. This lull is then unleashed into the barked chorus of "He's takin' Morphine!" which incorporates the sounds of the machinations of equipment used to help people breathe – specifically, it is a sample taken from David Lynch's movie *The Elephant Man*. It is the sound of the breathing apparatus Joseph Merrick needed to keep him alive.

The song featured on the 1997 release, *Blood On The Dance Floor*, which shifted over six million units and remains the biggest-selling remix album of all time. With this in mind, it seems reasonable to suggest that the song 'Morphine' must be the most vastly dismissed cry for help in all of history. Michael being vulnerable to relapsing into a drug habit was certainly no secret.

Indeed, during the *AEG* trial, Karen Faye testified about how, on the *Dangerous* tour, Michael's management kept him drugged up. Sony had set a new stipulation that required Michael to get a loan in order to finance the tour. He needed collateral, which was the catalogue. The Chandler allegations then derailed the tour, during which Michael was also fighting a plagiarism case (the harrowing video-taped deposition is unflinchingly graphic in its portrayal of Michael's suffering with pain). Michael went into rehab. In another taped deposition filmed years later, Michael talks about being so impaired by pain medication, that he can't remember whether or not he signed over power of attorney.

Ergo, Michael's painkiller habit was never rekindled on a whim.

The last time I saw Michael perform live was at the 1999 charity show *Michael Jackson and Friends*. (The event was subtitled 'What More Can I Give' after a song Michael had written before recording with a celebrity supergroup - the song was scuppered by Sony.)

During the event's rendition of 'Earth Song', the front part of the stage was elevated to create what Michael himself had titled 'The Bridge of No Return'. No return, indeed. The dramatic prop suddenly and swiftly collapsed, falling into the orchestra pit. But being the consummate professional he was, Michael spontaneously leapt from the debris to continue performing. Michael hurt his back so badly in the incident, that he returned to the solace of the analgesics he'd been treated with in the aftermath of the infamous burning he suffered filming for *Pepsi* in 1984.

I'm willing to concede - with regards the Estate's apparent attempt to sanitise Michael's soul - that the gruesome image offered up by the truth of the track 'Morphine' would certainly make for a particularly unpalatable cartoon.

But if Michael taught us anything, it is that – regardless – truth is always beautiful.

CHAPTER FOUR

For the lips of a strange woman drop as a honeycomb, and her mouth is smoother than oil.

PROVERBS 5:3

Mothers that have faith in their children ultimately see their faith qualified. Katherine had every faith in Michael, and the qualification is there for all to see. As Michael himself said, "All my success has been based on the fact that I wanted to make my mother proud, to win her smile and approval." Such immense love between a mother and son. The poetry Michael wrote for her; the album dedications; even the iconic song, 'The Way You Make Me Feel' - written for Katherine after she'd requested a song with a shuffling rhythm.

I remember a discussion I once had with a friend in 1993, when I was a teenager. The friend asked me if I thought Michael had written his best song yet, to which I replied that I didn't believe he had. I explained that I imagined his best was to come, because the grief he would feel when his mother died would stir in him an artistic expression at a level we hadn't hitherto witnessed. He wouldn't be able to help but write a song about it. As an artist – to try and manage the situation - it's what he would have had to do. Of course, Michael didn't live long enough to write that song about the bereavement of his mother. Though his sadness at the self-destructive nature of humanity towards Mother Nature provided us with an equivalent (it was a sad day indeed when Michael Jackson, of all people, was moved to record the words, "I used to dream / I used to glance beyond the stars / Now I don't know where we are / Although I know / We've drifted far").

Michael's adoration of his own mother is well documented, but in the foreword he contributed to a recipe book, he reveals an appreciation for the magical nature of motherhood in general:

"Remember when you were little and your mother made a pie for you? When she cut a slice and put it on your plate, she was giving you a bit of herself, in the form of her love. She made you feel safe and wanted. She made your hunger go away, and when you were full and satisfied, everything seemed all right... You may think that your apple pie has only sugar and spice in it. A child is wiser... with the first bite, he knows that this special dish is the essence of your love."

***

The theme of the femme fatale is a prominent one in Michael's work, something that led to accusations of his being misogynistic. This is a somewhat myopic perspective, as well as one easily discredited. Fundamentally – after all – the very idea of the femme fatale is one that acknowledges the power that women can wield.

During the 1984 *Grammy Awards* - when Michael was nominated for fourteen, before winning an unprecedented eight of them - upon accepting one of the gongs, there is a moment when Quincy Jones whispers in Michael's ear. Instantly, Michael turns back to the microphone and gives a shout-out to "the girls in the balcony". Later on in the ceremony - when Michael once again returns to the podium to collect another prize - Michael jokes about having made a deal with himself to remove his aviators if he went on to break the record for the number of *Grammy's* won in a single night. In what seems to be an afterthought, before taking off his glasses, Michael also dedicates the gesture to "the girls at the back."

Michael's sense of humility was on full display during his accepting of the awards, with him using the occasion to dedicate one of them – in inference, at least - to the unjustly maligned black musical luminary, Jackie Wilson. Michael also thanked Steven Spielberg for giving him the opportunity to work on the E.T. soundtrack, for which Michael won one of the *Grammy's*. Michael explained that he felt an affinity with the cinematic alien, by saying,

"He's in a strange place and wants to be accepted… He's most comfortable with children, and I have a great love for kids. He gives love and wants love in return, which is me. And he has that super power which lets him lift off and fly whenever he wants to get away from things on Earth, and I can identify with that. He and I are alike in many ways."

The *Thriller* album, for which Michael received the remaining seven accolades, features 'Lady In My Life' - a song saturated in sensuality. This track, however, was written by Rod Temperton. A more accurate portrayal of Michael's attitudes towards women and sexuality around this time are found in the self-penned pop soap opera, 'Billie Jean' and the *Thriller* outtake, 'Carousel' in which Michael references the naïve voyeuristic circus entertainment that was "Only your eyes for a dime".

Michael's companions that night were Brooke Shields and Emmanuel Lewis. Candid backstage footage of the event that was recently made public shows Michael, Brooke and Emmanuel in an elevator. Whilst the three are hidden from public view, Brooke is essentially ignored at the expense of Emmanuel. Though as soon as the elevator doors open, Michael once again takes Brooke's arm.

Michael's behaviour in the footage is certainly susceptible to close-minded and cynical judgement. Yet, it is important to bear in mind that at this juncture in Michael's life, it seems he purposely curtailed the gratification of his libido in an effort to concentrate on his primary focus – his galvanised career. Also – and no less significantly – Michael's apparent disinterest in sex at this point was perhaps a consequence of his uniquely peculiar upbringing: one that left him hesitant with regards to such matters. What with the mystifying messages that had bombarded his maturing psyche - the bewilderment of being torn between a profound loyalty to his venerated stay-at-home mother and her deeply religious views, and the negative contrast of a dedication to a life on the road in which witnessing behaviour of sexual immorality was par-for-course. Michael's precocious eyes were witnessing nightly the debauchery of the strip clubs that formed part of the *Jackson 5*'s promotional circuit, as well as the behaviours that were an inevitable consequence of sharing bedrooms in which his father and brothers entertained groupies. Michael's repulsion at the disrespect for his mother and in the treatment of said groupies, lends further support for his love of women in its own right.

Besides, Brooke and Michael remained close, regardless. In words disclosed by Rabbi Shmuley Boteach, Michael rues the day that Brooke attempted to get amorous with him, but he was too nervous to indulge:

"I sincerely liked Brooke, I liked her a lot. She was one of the loves of my life… I was at the *Academy Awards* with Diana Ross and she just came up to me and said: 'Hi, I'm Brooke Shields. Are you going to the after party?' I said: 'Yeah' and I just melted. So we get to the party and she says: 'Would you dance with me?' And we went on the dance floor. And man, we exchanged numbers and I was up all night, spinning around in my room, just happy. She was classy. We had one encounter when she got real intimate and I chickened out. And I shouldn't have"

Michael's friendship with Brooke survived longer than his relationship with Emmanuel did; with her regularly being seen accompanying Michael in the ensuing years. Similarly, once Michael's marriage with Lisa Marie Presley was over, they remained on good terms – with Lisa Marie frequently flying out to see Michael all over the world whilst he was on the road with the *HIStory* tour

***

In songs inspired by Jackson family dynamics, such as 'Superfly Sister' and 'Monkey Business', Michael laments some of the actions of certain members of his family. In the lyrics to the latter track, Michael bemoans the loose morals of the male members of his family, singing,

"Your brother's gone and kissed / The mother-in-law / I might tell dad about what I saw / Your brother didn't make a nickel or dime."

Michael's propensity for generalising a theme in order to appeal to a larger audience – such as in 'Leave Me Alone' – was second to none. But in 'Monkey Business' the glove is well and truly off, with the intended recipients of the message being perfectly clear. And although Michael switches between third and first person perspectives, in an effort to afford him the liberty of ambiguity – and therefore seeming less direct in his accusations – the subject matter of taking his family's indiscretions to task remained a courageous choice of his. The lyric "I might tell dad about what I saw" is instantly endearing in its childlikeness, and reveals a great deal about this facet of Michael's personality.

Though the song 'Superfly Sister' is in itself a direct rebuttal of sexist attitudes – a judgement on the superficial rating of women by men, with its repeated refrain reminding us that, "Push it in, stick it out / That ain't what it's all about" - Michael does not hold back in discriminating from highlighting his disappointment with some of the lifestyle choices of his siblings, irrelevant of their gender. As he sings,

"Susie like to agitate / Get the boy and make him wait / Mother's preaching Abraham / Brothers they don't give a damn."

Michael's love for his sisters was, nevertheless, very evident. He produced music with all three of his sisters, even giving the *Bad* album outtake 'Fly Away' to his eldest sister, Rebbie, for her 1998 album *Yours Faithfully* - as well as writing the track 'Centipede' for her. In the 1983 *Unauthorised* interview undertaken with LaToya, the effortless repartee between Michael and his sibling is there for all to see. In an interview a decade later, Oprah Winfrey asks Michael if he has read LaToya's 'tell-all' autobiography – to which he responds that he hasn't, because he doesn't need to, as he understands LaToya's true heart. It was this rational attitude that enabled Michael to forgive the misguided comments made by LaToya during the media frenzy of 1993. Michael understood that the essence of his sister was one of vulnerability, and that she had become a coerced and powerless victim of egregious abuse. This trait of vulnerability being a familial one – that would eventually contribute to Michael's ultimate demise.

Janet's steadfast backing of Michael throughout his tribulations is legendary. Not only did she team up with Michael to duet with him on his post-allegations comeback single, 'Scream', but also – with total disregard for the contemporaneous status of her career being at its zenith – chose to join Michael on stage to receive the song's *1995 MTV Video Music Award* for 'Best Dance Video'. Furthermore, not being content with the constraints of the effusive praise she could vocally bestow upon Michael as part of her stolid advocating of him, she brazenly wore a t-shirt bearing the words 'PERVERT 2' emblazoned across its back. You smear Michael, you smear Janet – was the very clear message.

Incidentally, Janet's infamous performance at the 2004 *Superbowl* half-time show - a result of which the expression 'wardrobe malfunction' was invented - marked the moment Janet's career was all-but terminated. The extent of opprobrium and malice Janet underwent as a consequence of the exposing of her breast is nothing short of bizarre. Justin Timberlake, on the other hand - the man Janet shared the stage with that night - has seen his career progress in leaps and bounds.

***

Michael intentionally chose a female guitarist to tour with him, with Jennifer Batten remaining a tour stalwart of his for a decade. There are a gamut of nuances in Michael's on-stage relationship with Jennifer that, due to their subtleties, perhaps offer a more genuine level of evidence for Michael's intrinsic respect for women than can be found anywhere else.

In the 'Dirty Diana' performance during one of the Wembley *Bad* tour shows, guest guitarist Steve Stevens – the musician on the record – is given "time to shine" (to use Michael's expression when he is emboldening *This Is It* guitarist, Orianthi - another musician specifically chosen with the intent of subverting gender stereotypes and making a statement in support of women). However, Michael is still seen at pains to ensure that the crowd recognise Jennifer's contribution as well as the guest performer's.

Jennifer herself gets her own "time to shine" during the sonically incongruous guitar solo she is gifted with for 'Working Day And Night'. The incongruity throws extra spotlight on Michael's unorthodox decision to employ the services of a woman in the role. The mutual fondness between Michael and Jennifer can be seen in footage of the 'Beat It' solo during the Copenhagen *HIStory* tour show. At its denouement, Michael seems slightly out of sorts, and as Jennifer exits stage-left and Michael gives her an affirmative pat of gratitude, Jennifer responds by providing Michael with a reassuring nudge. A nightly-repeated dance move of Michael's during the 'Beat It' solo was a crouched toe-stand, the successful conclusion for which – in order to maintain his centre of balance – meant having to hold onto Jennifer's leg for support.

One of Michael's later 'femme fatale' works was 'Blood On The Dance Floor'. The short film for the track features Michael in the role of a pimp, and borrows its theme from the cinematic interpretation of Georges Bizet's opera, *Carmen* – the tale of the archetypal seductress. The imagery evoked in 'Blood On The Dance Floor', in which 'Susie' "stuck seven inches in" and Michael asks, "Since you seduced her / How does it feel / To know that woman / Is out to kill?" was interpreted by some commentators as a sexist reference to promiscuous women and their role in the spread of HIV/AIDS – an idea immediately rebuffed by Michael. However, it would be disingenuous of me - considering my stance on the criminal ubiquity of the discrediting of the subtleties in Michael's art – to dismiss this interpretation outright. But one need only look to 'Smooth Criminal' or 'Little Susie' for evidence of Michael's penchant for a dark lyrical narrative. Though both of those examples comprise of Michael's concern for his central female characters.

This concern for the female protagonist is also apparent in his songs that feature prostitutes. Michael empathises with the plight of the 'streetwalker', and makes an effort to expose the reasons for their finding themselves in such desperate circumstances. The narratives of 'Do You Know Where Your Children Are' ("The police come 'round the corner / Somebody up there had told / He's arresting this little girl / Who's only twelve years old") and 'Hollywood Tonight' ("She's giving hot tricks to men… / When she was taught that that's not clean / Because she's only fifteen") both involve girls having to resort to prostitution in order to survive. The lyrics of 'Slave to the Rhythm' regale a tale in which Michael worries about gender inequality, and the everyday injustices suffered by women at the hands of patriarchy.

***

Michael had an uncanny knack for incorporating trademarks into his transient physicality: the single white glove; the sunglasses; the arm-brace; the mask; the umbrella – all props that were essential byproducts necessitated by his changing physical appearance.

(Although the single white glove also served the dual purpose of highlighting Michael's moves as he danced – as did the white socks. As he explained, "I love to accent movement. The eye goes to where the white is - you know, the glove.")

For the *Dangerous* campaign, Michael focussed in on his next image - becoming thicker-set as he matured. For the 'In The Closet' short film, he hired the services of Herb Ritts, renowned for raunchy photography. He hired John Singleton, fresh from *Boyz in the Hood*, to direct the 'Remember The Time' video, which featured an all-black cast (including, on Michael's insistence, a role for the basketball star Magic Johnson, who had recently publicly revealed his being HIV-positive). The 1993 *Grammy's* speech Michael gave - upon receiving the *Grammy Legend Award* - was meant as a reset button for all the bizarre behaviour of the eighties. Michael - he claimed - hadn't "been aware that the world thought [he] was so weird", and announced that he had undergone a "rebirth". The promotional drive behind *Dangerous* was to portray Michael as mature and sexy, whilst also reclaiming any black support he may have lost during the *Bad* era.

An all-out attack ensued to convince anyone sceptical about Michael's heterosexuality. The 'Give In To Me' and 'Who Is It' short films are loaded with sexual connotations (the lyrics to 'Give In To Me' have been interpreted by some as alluding to rape); and the 'Remember The Time' promo - to much chatter at the time - featured Michael's first on-screen kiss (with David Bowie's wife - the pulchritudinous Nubian model Iman - becoming the much-envied recipient, in her role as Pharaohess). However, such subtleties were flagrantly dismissed with for the 'In The Closet' short film, in which Michael's interactions with Naomi Campbell are intimate, to say the least (particularly in pictures taken during rehearsals, where Michael's enthusiasm for incorporating the suggested stimulation of Naomi's – let's say 'groin' – into a proposed dance move, completely belie the myth of a shyness with women in his more mature years).

Candid footage of Michael in his forties portrays him as very much the heterosexual man. During film shot in the back of cars that are swarmed with baying fans, Michael is seen excitedly commenting on the attractiveness of some of the girls, who he liked to call "Fish". In other footage, filmed when Michael was given free reign of a supermarket (an opportunity granted upon his request to experience something resembling normality) - in between riding around the aisles on a trolley - Michael picks up a magazine adorned with the image of his friend Elizabeth Taylor, then turns to hold the picture towards the camera, before smiling coyly, and saying "Now *that's* what I'm talking about!"

***

In a 1972 interview, **Michael was asked** about singing love songs at such a young age, to which he responded, "It's not odd for me to sing love songs because I know what I'm singing about… There's no age limit to love."

It seems the confused, young Michael precociously crooned about romantic and erotic love in an effort to please one of his mentors in particular. Whilst, in the one hand, his father held the stick of motivation, in the other, the dazzling Diana Ross, held the carrot. The relationship between Michael and Diana lasted his entire life, with Diana named in the will as a guardian for his children. One need only glance at footage of Michael in his early twenties, invited on stage by Diana to duet with her on the track 'Upside Down' to be convinced of the sexual chemistry between them. This is also seen during the 1996 *World Music Awards*, in which, during her performance, Diana positions herself in Michael's lap, whilst he is sat enthralled by her on the front row. The theory that Michael's heartbreak at the hands of Diana is what spurred his success in the eighties - as if he were trying to prove himself worthy of her - is certainly a feasible one. Especially when it's considered that heartbreak was a huge motivating force for Michael – the heartbreak of lost childhood being his primary muse in the latter years of his career. And although Michael's song 'Dirty Diana' concerns the actions of groupies, his choice to use that name in particular remains intriguing.

'Liberian Girl' was originally entitled 'Pyramid Girl', and was written around the time Michael forged a friendship with Elizabeth Taylor.

It's not such a stretch to imagine that Michael fell in love with - and was hence inspired by - Taylor's role in the movie *Cleopatra*, based in Egypt. Michael dedicated 'Remember The Time' to Diana Ross, and 'Liberian Girl' to Elizabeth Taylor. And – indisputably - both were significant loves in his life. Though forming conclusions on Michael's loves on the basis of his song dedications is by no means an infallible method. With one only needing to note the person Michael dedicated 'Blood On The Dance Floor' to, in order for the system to be thrown into confusion. What with that particular commendation being granted to none other than Sir Elton John.

The paradox that was Michael being the most well-known person on the planet, yet feeling like the loneliest, is not a difficult one to comprehend. The fact that he was so loved became the very reason he himself couldn't find love. The times he felt genuine love where from children, and from audiences. Potential partners flocked around him from all over the globe. Anywhere he visited, he had his pick of opportunities for romance. And it was precisely this automatic love for him that made it so difficult for him to discern sincerity. Millions of people remain in love with him without ever having met him. Think what it was like for all those people that did meet him. Sycophancy – well-meaning or otherwise - became a curse for Michael. Michael's second wife, Debbie Rowe, loved Michael so much she volunteered to carry his children, before handing them over as a no-ties gift.

The difficulties Michael underwent in finding sincere romantic love - considering the constancy of people throwing themselves wantonly at his feet - was akin to someone searching for the radiance of Sirius whilst standing in the blinding beam of sunlight. It meant that such was the magnitude of Michael's own brilliance as the brightest superstar, he also became the most distant.

During the *Bad* era, Michael was linked to Tatiana Thumbtzen - the model who appeared in the 'The Way You Make Me Feel' video – even joining Michael on tour to perform on stage with him during the live version of the song. One night, Thumbtzen had the audacity to kiss Michael on stage. This behaviour was frowned upon by Michael's management, and she was swiftly replaced. It seemed Michael's handlers were under the impression that their cash cow could do without such distractions. In the *Bad* album outtake 'Price Of Fame', Michael laments his position, singing,

"I was excited about the way that things could have been… / They started taking pictures, autographs, then they grab / My joy had turned to pain".

***

The latterday examples that suggest the truth of Michael's sexual orientation have an irrefutable sincerity about them. But there are also many quotes taken during the *Jackson 5* years, in which all the brothers' hot-blooded-male credentials are apparently cemented. One such supposed citation from Michael being, "I have this weakness – I love looking at girls!'"

However, it would be further disingenuous of me to promote such quotes as being the verbatim thoughts of a teenage Michael. In the same way Michael and his brothers were coached with regards portraying a benign stance on issues such as black rights for the sake of commercial potentiation, so they also were in context of their views on their female fanbase. Nonetheless, the idea of the dubious credibility of such quotes is fascinating in itself. The practice of public perspectives on Michael's sexuality being enforced by pedantic and paranoid profiteers, solely concerned with the palatability of his image, was a system heavy with repercussions for the person that would become the adult Michael Jackson.

This entrenched understanding that Michael had of public relations became the reason he was so careful – and so clever – when it came to camouflaging the political messages contained in his later work. Michael understood it was merely a matter time before people unveiled the messages in his art. To have managed this tight-rope so expertly with such faith in the long-game, was a manifestation of startling genius.

Perhaps counterintuitively, to find the ultimate proof of Michael's perspective on women, one need look no further than his face. It was a face that he had initially wanted to be seen adorned with lace for the cover of the *Bad* album – a desire overruled by his record company, who took it to the other extreme, and insisted on a relatively macho image of Michael instead. Far from being misogynistic, Michael elevated femininity to the extent that he was completely comfortable in androgenising himself – he voluntarily absorbed the feminine into his appearance.

Michael viewed himself as a visionary: a sincere and plausible surmising borne as a consequence of his having been a uniquely positioned observer in the spiritual evolution of humanity. For a third-of-a-century, his career had entailed entertaining hundreds of millions of souls brought together as a result of love. There exists an interesting correlation between Michael's unshackling himself of the craving for commercial success in favour of philanthropic achievements, and his acquiescence in allowing himself opportunities to succeed in romantic love. Though Michael effortlessly stirred millions of women into maniacal frenzies, the phenomenon of his fainting fanhood became by no means an exclusively female occurrence. As Michael said,

"But I am finding today, and it is so true, that guys today are really changing and I have watched it happen through my career. Guys scream with the same kind of adulation that girls do in a lot of countries. They are not ashamed."

Michael had witnessed the change in behaviour of male fans over the decades he had been performing. He witnessed in real-time the increasing confidence of people celebrating the emancipated self. Michael had intuited society's increasing intolerance of paternalistic orthodoxy. Archaic attitudes that he so sublimely subverted himself in his total reconstruction of the stereotypical family unit.

This was Michael's power.

CHAPTER FIVE

By the power of truth, I, while living, have conquered the universe.

THEODOR REUSS

"I am Michael Jackson now."

- The very words John Branca, Co-executor of the Estate of Michael Jackson, was purported to have uttered upon Michael's death. Words so drenched in disdain that they could neither be more offensive nor telling in their outright dismissal of the feelings of Michael's legion of adoring and loyal fans.

It is fortunate that Michael was so adept at spinning, considering the number of times this claim must have caused him to turn in his grave.

Michael's relationship with Sony Music forged another unfortunate area in which he became embroiled in politics and conspiracy theory. Upon the release of 2001's *Invincible* and its relatively substandard commercial success, Michael commenced a campaign to expose his belief in the duplicity of the chief of Sony Music at the time, Tommy Mottola - who Michael described as "the devil". This discontent with Sony Music had been slow-burning, with Michael gradually perceiving that whenever he attempted to use his art to express his feeling of being victimised at the hands of the establishment, the project would suffer from poor promotion and distribution (such as in the short film *Ghosts* - co-written with horror-connoisseur Stephen King, directed by special effects supremo Stan Winston and premiered at the 1997 *Cannes Film Festival*). The conundrum of this anti-political-Michael tactic continued to be observed with the release of posthumous box sets and compilations - which would feature all of his albums, except for the polemic second disc of the *HIStory* album. In spite of the record's status as the biggest-selling double album of all time.

Michael was no stranger to putting his hand in his pocket to fund his work - having self-financed much of the production of the timeless 'Beat It' and 'Thriller' promos - and hence felt unfairly treated by not being met half-way by a record company for whom he had made so many billions of dollars.

Indeed, in the short film for the initial single release from *Invincible*, 'You Rock My World' the first words uttered by Michael are, "I'm not payin' for it... You're the one who wanted to cover it - not me... You wanted to cover it."

Michael hadn't wanted 'You Rock My World' as the first release from *Invincible*. This meant that the short film became an eleventh-hour panic production, manifesting as an amalgamation of themes from his music video canon. Albeit with added political references to Michael's grievances with losing creative control to Tommy Motolla. In protest, Michael covered his face for the majority of the short film, and wore a Cripps-inspired bandana beneath his fedora, whilst symbolically dancing in front of a 'No Checks Cashed' sign and smashing a 'No Fighting' sign. One of the henchmen Michael is confronted by, insidiously snarls that he thinks that Michael "wants to die". Another wields a Frank Dileo-esque cigar.

There is actual physical fighting, as opposed to earlier works in which dance-offs were Michael's preferred medium to settle a score (bar his gun-toting turn in the 'Smooth Criminal' video. However, Michael had been bullied for long enough, and had endured it with saint-like dignity and patience. He had earned the right to lash out. Albeit, still in an artistic and studied fashion (Michael's punch is disguised as a dance move). The choice to use unprovoked violence in an effort to demonstrate superiority merely undermines those that opt for it, due to it being an act of insecurity at its very essence. Bullies live in terror of their victims' realisation that they are weak. Losing control of their prey is out of the question. Bullies need so much love. As Michael said, "You ain't bad - you ain't nuthin'!"

At the short film's denouement, Michael and Marlon Brando – who else? – briefly exchange ambiguities, as the bar in which this has all been taking place is consumed by fire. Michael says to Brando, "I know who you are." To which Brando replies, "Bing bang… Later."

Michael considered the lack of financial support for *Invincible*, along with his having to cede artistic decisions to men in suits, as once again indicative of counterproductive tactics being undertaken by his record company. Sony had allegedly claimed Michael owed them $200 million in production costs, to which Michael replied, "For Sony to make a false claim that I owe them $200 million is outrageous and offensive."

With regards *Invincible*, Michael had the last laugh. The album debuted at number one in thirteen countries, before selling over thirteen million copies as it intermittently re-entered worldwide music charts throughout the noughties. At the end of which, it was hailed as *Album of the Decade* in a 2010 *Billboard* poll.

***

John Branca's ongoing stewardship of the Estate has overseen many controversial choices.

The vast majority of fan consensus these days accepts that three tracks on *Michael* - the first posthumous album of 'new' material released after the Estate's $250 million deal with Sony Music (the only company Michael ever overtly campaigned against) - are performed by an imposter. Said tracks are 'Breaking News', 'Keep Your Head Up' and 'Monster'.

Every member of Michael's family who has publicly commented on these tracks has also made the same claim as most of Michael's fans - that they believe the tracks are fake. Even Michael's grieving daughter took to Twitter to confirm her belief that all of the Cascio songs were bogus.

One day - the story goes - Michael decided to visit his friends' house and record these three remarkably subpar songs in the style of a sound-alike. Not only that, Michael chose to then further experiment by singing said songs through a piece of pipe. Whilst he stood in the shower.

This remains the official explanation for the reason that the now-notorious 'Cascio' tracks do not sound like Michael.

Three decades ago, Paul McCartney released his *Pipes Of Peace* album, upon which resides the songs 'Say Say Say' and 'The Man' - two irrefutably majestic vocal duets between McCartney and Michael. The song was one of three written by the two artists during a fertile period of collaboration, with the other being 'The Girl Is Mine', which featured on Michael's *Thriller* album – the song being a sing-off further demonstrating the unparalleled prowess of the two vocalists. In spite of the title of the *Pipes Of Peace* album, I'm not aware of any rumours suggesting either Michael or Paul sang through pipes on the track. I'm not sure when Michael decided to start singing through pipes, but I certainly consider the adoption of this technique to have been a mistake. Because - on the 'Cascio' tracks - it makes Michael sound much less like he had one of the richest, unique and most soulful singing voices in all history - one nurtured and nuanced by determined industry since early childhood - and much more like he's engaging in spontaneous, drunken, self-parodying, rage karaoke.

Over the past thirty years, ever since the *Pipes Of Peace* album was published, I have listened to Michael's voice every single day. As a working estimate - although it's certainly more - I have listened to Michael singing around 100,000 times. I have heard his voice mature; I have heard his style change. Say what you like about my plainly evident morbidly-obsessive, borderline-autistic behaviour, but you have to admit, I'm probably a bit of an expert on what his voice sounds like. I could tell you with 100% accuracy which hiccup, yelp or "hee hee" comes from which song.

In 2006, *Access Hollywood* conducted Michael's last televised interview. It was undertaken in Ireland during his nomadic period. During the interview, Michael demonstrates his notoriously fastidious attention to detail regarding his music – explaining how he puts each sound "under the microscope."

This trait for aspiring to perfection was yet further evidenced in a picture recently made public that shows a note Michael left for producer Jimmy Jam saying, "…the part I'm hearing for our chorus is the same sound you used on the bridge to the 'Knowledge'. The wind kind sound. Talk to me about this when I return to the studio."

There is also a point further on in the *Access Hollywood* footage, in which the interviewer infers that Justin Timberlake - later employed by Sony Music to perform on a posthumous duet with Michael - is the contemporaneous popular musical artist most responsible for continuing Michael's legacy. Michael quickly retorts that we shouldn't neglect to include the black artist, Usher, on the list.

There is a YouTube montage that demonstrates Michael's remarkable capacity for beatboxing, how he could effortlessly synthesise breath and pulse into a sublime musical experience. Michael's use of harmonies, where he painstakingly took it upon himself to provide both immaculate lead, as well as layer upon layer of backing vox, represent examples of the art form at its most sublime. It's hard to find a musical or emotional adjective which Michael hadn't mastered to a superlative standard. He used his voice as effectively as a drum as he did a harp, to convey everything from anger to whimsy. Take some time to appreciate the verses of the *Dangerous* track, 'Can't Let Her Get Away'. Hear how the chord progression reflects his angst.

Michael was a bona fide genius. His desire for immortality was pedantically worked into his craft. As he said himself, "To escape death I attempt to bind my soul to my work because I just want it to live forever."

Hence, the wince-inducing lyrical drivel the Cascio brothers managed to muster in an attempt to pass off work worthy of Michael, is insulting to say the least. Their lyric, "Mama say mama got you in a zig zag" appears to be some egregious effort to reference the chant "mamase mamasa makossa" from 'Wanna Be Startin' Somethin''. Never mind that this coda, used to such iconic effect by Michael, was actually a thought-out inclusion to the track, with the chant being part of the traditional Cameroonian ritual performed by women before losing their virginity to their husbands-to-be. (Though, admittedly, it's difficult to discern where Michael's lyric "You're a vegetable" from the same song fits into it all.)

Add all this to the abject disrespect shown for the very real road to perdition that Michael was forced to travail at the hands of the media, with the theme being so condescendingly taken advantage of in the clichéd lyrics to 'Breaking News' - and the flagrant endeavour to undermine Michael's legacy for a swift and cynical profit feels complete.

It's open to speculation as to why Sony Music decided to press ahead with the steadfast promulgation of tracks deemed bogus. But a prominent theory is that after having done a deal to release seven albums over ten years, they discovered that - for whatever reason - there simply aren't enough songs in the vault, and hence need to flesh the albums out using music featuring an imposter. Another theory is that the treatment of Michael's legacy is a systematic attempt to manipulate a situation in which the Estate has no remaining financial option but to sell its half of Michael's precious music catalogue to the owners of the other half, Sony Music. Whatever the reason, what is evident is that Sony Music aren't so much milking everything possible out of their most profitable cash cow, as they are maniacally bludgeoning its bones into unrecognisable bits. They are not so much flogging a dead horse as, well… you get the picture.

"I am the Edison phonograph… I can sing you tender songs of love. I can give you merry tales and joyous laughter. I can transport you to the realms of music. I can cause you to join in the rhythmic dance. I can lull the babe to sweet repose, or waken in the aged heart soft memories of youthful days."

Michael sampled part of this quote for his song, 'HIStory'. It is from the world's first ever record: a revolution that gave the world not only the miracle of recorded music, but with it, the accompanying, less-virtuous aspect of recorded advertisement, with its associated capitalist traits of hoodwinking and greed. The Edison phonograph was an invention of awe and wonder at the time - though the sound quality wasn't like it is these days.

Even so, it's a safe bet that Michael's fans would have still been able to distinguish the sound of his voice from that of an imposter. As Michael prophetically expressed through the rap borrowed from the Notorious B.I.G. for 'Unbreakable', "How can players stand there and say I sound like them, HELLO?!"

Amongst the other historically significant soundbites that Michael incorporated into the outro for the track, 'HIStory', is one of himself as a child, in which he states, "I don't sing it if I don't mean it".

The ruthless duplicity exhibited by the producers of the Cascio tracks is shown in how it seems they merely aimed for an imposter to sound just enough like Michael to the layperson, in order to make any legal challenge difficult.

In 'Strength Of One Man', a song that features on the eponymous *The Jacksons* album, the brothers sing,

"We have picked people that say they're on our side / And after they did everything they want / They start to tell us lie, just lie after lie."

The tenderness with which these lyrics are sung demonstrate clearly for just how long Michael and his family have had problems with being able to trust people.

Trust is a trait with double edges. A misguided trust in the goodness of all people brought Michael both unbridled love from his fans, as well as acts of malevolence from those jealous of his successes or covetous of his catalogue. Not that this malevolence was always overt, far from it. As Michael said, after his rude awakening, "There are people out there who don't actively hold you back as much as they work quietly on your insecurities so that you hold yourself back."

Indeed, there exists some candid footage of Michael being secretly filmed by a 'friend'. The person behind the camera asks Michael what the greatest lesson he's learned is. To which he replies, "Not to trust everybody."

The *Michael* debacle has by no means been the sum of the Estate's perceived ineptitude. Fans believe there is a veritable litany of examples of their being unfit for purpose.

***

Remember the hypocrisy demonstrated by the Estate's pursuit of damages from a Japanese man, who had been using Michael's image and likeness on items such as lighters and keyrings? The Estate released a statement regarding the case,

"Michael loved his millions of Japanese fans, all of whom deserve the opportunity to purchase legitimate and authentic Michael Jackson goods."

Even if we bring ourselves to temporarily disregard their previous endorsement of an apparent imposter in the music, this seemingly incongruent commercial cogency is further exposed by the Estate failing to act, in anyway whatsoever, in putting a stop to costume-designer Michael Bush's penchant for allegedly forging a Michael signature on hundreds of items marked for auction. Even on items that were produced after Michael's death.

Furthermore, one can only assume that the Estate sued the Japanese counterfeiter for a mere $2,150 – perhaps a few bootlegged tea-towels and fridge magnets worth – as this is what they themselves valued Michael's image at in their tax return. In comparison - to put this massive undervaluation into context - the image and likeness of Bob Marley is valued at two billion dollars. John Branca is a highly adept and experienced lawyer. It seems unusual, to say the least, that he has managed to preside over the Estate accruing a three-quarter-of-a-billion dollar tax deficit bill.

Then there was *Xscape*.

The humiliation and degradation of Michael continued in the production of an album that followed up one bearing just his first name, with one that eradicated his name entirely. None of the three albums released posthumously by Sony Music and the Estate bear an actual image of Michael – even the silhouette that adorns *This Is It* is posed by an impersonator – yet Michael was the most photographed person that has ever existed. (And people still ponder why he had issues with his self-image).

Xscape – a paltry one-and-a-half-million copies sold - was promoted using a 'hologram' gimmick of a Michael lookalike. (Not a hologram of Michael. A hologram of a lookalike.) A homogenised digital puppet programmed to perform at the 2014 *Billboard Awards*. This baffling decision evokes the famous words of Sam Phillips - the owner of Elvis' first record label, *Sun Records* - "If I could find a white boy who could sing like a black man I'd make a million dollars."

It also brings to mind Michael's own words,

"Record companies steal, they cheat, you have to audit them and it's time for artists to take a stand against them because they totally take advantage of them. They forget that it's the artists who make the company, not the company who makes the artists. Without the talent, the company would be nothing but just hardware. It takes real good talent. That's what the public wants to see."

The reason Sony Music gave for the relative commercial failure of the *Invincible* album, was that Michael had lost his appeal. Michael's response was to organise protests, during which he held aloft signs that read, "Sony Kills Music", "Sony Sucks" and "Sony Is Phony" atop an open double decker bus.

Once Michael was dead, however, it appears that Sony Music had a change of heart, and decided there was actually quite a lot of money yet to be mulched out of his name. And thus commenced a massive advertising assault in order to garner it. Who could have guessed that the zombie reanimation of Michael in the 'Thriller' video would prove to be so prophetic?

The tag-lines that accompanied the *Xscape* album's promotion were: "The Best You've Never Heard" - which could only have been a sarcastic allusion to the fact that seventy-five percent of the track-listing consisted of lovingly bastardised versions of demo tracks that had been online for up to eleven years; and, "Hearing Is Believing" - which could only have been a sarcastic allusion to the 'Cascio' fiasco.

In the song 'Xscape', Michael is heard taunting his pursuers with the words, "You want me? Come and get me!" And get him, they did.

As part of the *Xscape* project, the Estate signed a deal with Sony Music to promote their smartphone, the *Xperia* (also starts with an 'X' – get it?), in which the album would be exclusively included as part of the package, upon purchase of the phone. The Estate also signed a deal with car manufacture *Jeep*, who then employed the 'contemporised' version of 'Love Never Felt So Good' in an advertisement. Further, they then had one of their cars prominently featured in the video for the single 'A Place With No Name' (never mind that a lyric in the song concerns a Jeep breaking down). This 'contemporised' version of 'A Place With No Name' shamelessly incorporates the chords from Michael's privacy-plea song – you couldn't make this up – 'Leave Me Alone'.

A minor victory resulting from the fan furore at the censoring of the lyrics to the *Michael* track 'Hollywood Tonight' (in which the removal of the words "Because she's only fifteen" simultaneously sanitised the song of all context) was Sony Music's subsequent decision for the *Xscape* release to include the controversial aspects of the song 'Do You Know Where Your Children Are' - in which Michael emotes from the perspective of a prostituted twelve-year-old girl, with the words, "Save me from this living hell... 'cos I'm terrified."

The *Xscape* track 'Blue Gangster' is heavy with poignancy, with its lyric, "Look what you done to me? / I can no longer smile", and the inherent despair comprising the "Aaah aaah aah" of the bridge being tangible.

***

It should go without saying that Michael would have been less than happy with the posthumous tinkering of his art. As he said in 1980,

"I do believe deeply in perfection. I'm never satisfied… If you're just satisfied with anything, you're just going to stay at one level and the world will move ahead."

For many, however, it was not even the principle of Sony Music releasing songs that Michael was unsatisfied with and had deemed unready to add to his historically unique canon of work. It was more the very idea of Sony Music accumulating wealth off Michael's back, when he had strived and suffered for so long to be rid of their shackles. As Michael mused,

"I could never just make records for people to buy and just get rich from. That's no good for me. There has to be more than that… I try to write, put it in song. Put it in dance. Put it in my art to teach the world. If politicians can't do it, I want to do it. We have to do it.

Artists, put it in paintings. Poets, put it in poems, novels. That's what we have to do. And I think it's so important to save the world."

Michael cried upon discovering how much longer he had to endure on his contract with Sony Music; and he whooped with joy when it finally drew to a close. On notes he made just prior to his death, Michael wrote about contacting Universal or Warner Bros. for a future record deal. He had spent an entire decade of his life trying to emancipate himself from Sony Music's chains, only for him then to have an image of his head photoshopped posthumously - for the *Xscape* album artwork - into what is reminiscent of the collars used to restrain flea-ridden dogs. The inspiration for this artwork apparently being drawn from a photo-shoot that Michael did with Arno Bani, in which he is portrayed as a Pharaoh. Though Michael was so unhappy with the resulting pictures, he requested that they be burned.

In 2003, upon discovering that John Branca was representing both him and Sony Music at the same time, Michael instructed his then-lawyer David LeGrand to terminate John Branca's employment contract. Such a conflict of interest would be undesirable in the best of scenarios - never mind one in which Michael was concurrently campaigning against Sony Music. It is therefore an understandable bugbear of the fan community, that upon the untimely death of Michael, Mr. Branca was announced as executor of his Estate. Branca thus became the executor of a will within which Michael's name is incorrect; his children's names are incorrect; and Michael's handwritten, time-stamped signature was ostensibly scribed in Los Angeles, albeit at a time and date that freely available video evidence proves Michael was three thousand miles away, at the other end of the United States. In New York. Protesting against Sony Music.

How could Michael be simultaneously signing charge of his posthumous assets over to John Branca in both New York and Los Angeles, at the very same minute, at the very same hour, on July 7, 2002?

Fan conversation often refers to Michael as having superhero qualities. We had been hitherto unaware that teleportation was one of them.

Other indiscrepancies, beyond the practicalities behind the signing of the will, and questions concerning the employment of an imposter in the attempt to pull the wool over fans' ears for improper profit, also need resolving.

The reason given by the Estate for not adhering to the 20% charitable donation stipulation of the will, is that the Estate's first responsibility was to take Michael out of debt. Yet, biggest-selling posthumous artist - with the largest-ever-grossing concert film and *Cirque du Soleil* world tour - later, the donations remain to be borne out. Although an unpaid three-quarter-of-a-billion dollar tax bill – a result of the Estate valuing Michael's half of the ATV Catalogue at $0 (I wonder what Sony Music value their half to be?) – has been.

Katherine Jackson's request for an audit was dismissed out of hand.

For what it's worth, Estate attorney Howard Weitzman did respond to the will-signing anomaly. He explained that the signatories must have simply forgotten where they were.

***

Apostles of Capitalism adopt the poignant messages of our heroes, then twist them into throwaway slogans with which to sell their wares. With CGI, it is all-too easy to insert a long-dead icon into an advert. It's a technique that is becoming increasingly ubiquitous. How long before we see a commercial for plastic surgery featuring a computer-generated Michael telling us to, "Make that change"?!

The attempted caricaturisation of Michael continues apace. The memory of the human being known as a record-breaking philanthropist and catalytic culture converter is being systematically reduced to pyrite falsities, through schemes that lure us into lining the pockets of already filthy-rich men, as if we are all whorish, turncoat magpies. Michael is their golden calf; but to us, he is the rotating ox:

he is our homecoming and food. It is materialism versus spiritual nourishment. It is soul versus sequins. We are the curators of Michael's legacy, and deceitful songs in his discography is a fundamentally unacceptable situation. And it will take the stamina and stoicism of warriors to remain focussed in our fight. The importance of curating Michael's legacy to an exemplary standard is revealed when considering that a legacy ferments. It ferments in myth and truth.

As Michael continued, in *The Jacksons* track, 'Strength of One Man',

"Now we can't blame our problems/ On just that chosen few / Cause if we wanna solve them / It's up to me and it's up to you."

It's perhaps ironic that I haven't listened to or seen anything of the posthumous 'Immortal' campaign. But therein that irony lies the crux of the matter. Michael's immortality lies in his artistry, not in how he is marketed. Michael fiercely guarded the integrity of the artists in the ATV catalogue, be they *The Beatles* or Little Richard. What right does big corporation have to not now afford him the same level of respect? Michael is being turned into a cartoon character; becoming even more of a commodity than he was when alive.

There are innumerable unsung black artists who wrote songs merely to feed the success and wealth of racist record companies, that preferred a white face to sell their records and make them money.

This is the very same racism that resonates in the hypocrisy manifest in the mockery of Michael's efforts to coalesce the world into harmony through music; a mockery that is in stark contrast to the vaunted statuses of the output of white counterparts, such as John Lennon (and, incidentally, in their vicious recriminations of Michael's bare-faced cheek in buying the rights to *The Beatles* catalogue).

Michael got up on stage in 2002 and called the contemporaneous head of Sony Music, Tommy Motolla, a racist. Sony Music responded to this, not by chastising their so-called washed-up artist, Michael Jackson, but by firing Motolla, their CEO. It makes one wonder what Michael might have had over them to nudge them into that decision. It's certainly difficult to believe that - upon the departure of Tommy Motolla - everything was suddenly resolved between Michael and Sony Music.

In 2002, as a black member on the board of Sony Music, Michael blew the whistle and told the world what was happening at the company. Fast forward thirteen years to the present day, and we are amidst the hacked email scandal exposing some Sony executives as harbouring racist views. These events vindicate Michael's accusations entirely.

Not for the last time will Michael's mantra, "Lies run sprints, but the truth runs marathons" become realised.

***

There is a divinity in devotion. And by devotion, I don't mean blind loyalty. On the contrary, to fully appreciate and love someone is to do so unconditionally, in spite of their recognised flaws. Michael was human. He was not perfect. But he believed that nothing was beyond hope if it could be bombarded with love; and it was his insistence on these idealistic beliefs – and in the use of his great power to promote these beliefs - that was surely divinely inspired.

As fans, it is vital to remember that we should not let our devotion be taken advantage of, and be capitalised upon. It is a testament to Michael's invincibility that his posthumous albums are promoted with all the hype as if he were still alive – which other artist gets that treatment? – but it is our devotion to his wishes as a humanitarian, and the preservation of the iconic art that he signed off himself that keeps Michael alive, not the success of a marketing campaign focussed solely on turning a profit for the people mismanaging his accounts.

Michael's very soul went into his artistic response to being labelled a child molester. Yet, the Estate are bewilderingly inefficient when it comes to defending Michael from more recent accusations: strangely refusing to engage with the hero Mr. Thomas Mesereau, Michael's esteemed attorney from the 2005 trial.

The 2014 resurfacing of slanderous stories involving Michael and children offered the slavering tabloid junkies nothing new: merely being rehashed, tired tactics that smacked so recognisably of newspapers in 1993; plucked from the ether and attributed to 'a source'. Reading their descriptions was akin to listening to someone detail the character of a mutual friend, a person you have known for decades, but who they have only recently become acquainted with. You know this old friend inside-out: their flaws; their tribulations; their virtues – and are therefore dumbfounded by the inaccuracy of this other person's depiction of them.

Sony Music have invested too much in their sanitised reinterpretation of Michael for them to allow it to be 'inconvenienced'. For better or worse, they understand that Michael is an industry unto himself – one that provides an opportunity for decades of profit-procurement – and the likelihood is that Sony Music will encourage the Estate to settle the 2014 claims out of court. Sony Music are extremely powerful, and have form – they misadvised Michael back in 1993, when they recommended he settle then.

And Sony Music may well have invested their money in Michael; but we have invested our hearts. We followed him devoutly as he vindicated himself in 2005, and we will not allow our decades of stoic support to be undermined by extortionists. Michael gladly assumed his responsibility as a gatekeeper for innocence. But, noticing that one has responsibilities is the easy part. Engaging with them is an altogether separate matter. It is our responsibility to engage in the defence of our voiceless hero against the ongoing systematic attempts at his vilification.

It is us that will decide if they are doing justice to our devotion.

The battle for Michael's historical integrity has many fronts. With the defence of the unparalleled capacity for his art to be used as a tool in making the world a better place being as ferocious an argument as any. As loyal fans, we must always bear in mind, that the title 'artist' is first and foremost the appellation Michael spent decades trying to earn; not 'commodity'. Let us not be distracted by the substandard dollar-generating shiny things the Estate dangle before us. We must never forget that it is us who are responsible, through our support of the Estate or lack thereof, for the quality control of Michael's legacy and his humanitarian reputation.

What do we want Michael's fame to become? What is our duty as fans? As human beings? Is it to mindlessly promote the current Estate's trend of him as a money-making vacuity? Or is it to enrich his reputation and memory through the promulgation of him as a politically-conscious, peace-loving leader? One whose mission was prematurely terminated by the very same nefarious ideals motivating the people now making millions off his name? Do we want to see him immortalised as a caricature of twentieth century pop culture and capitalism? Or as a talisman for peace, hope and mutual appreciation? In short: do we want him cartoonified or beatified?

As much as the Estate continue to insist on this cartoonification of Michael, the fans' reaction must be to further exalt him - that with their every insistence on insulting, they merely fortify his martyrdom. We must counteract with equal might. Michael was a totem; a conduit for the divine. He understood sacrifice as aspirational. He willingly sacrificed himself. Not only did he tour the planet a sick man, rescuing his reputation from slanderous smears whilst simultaneously promoting his message of peace; not only did he later die attempting to do the same thing; but throughout his adult life he used his abyss of self, a tragic side-effect of a pillaged childhood, to construct a mirror for humanity. He gave us the opportunity to reflect upon him.

He was the mirror in the man.

John Branca's time at the helm is bound to ephemerality. It is us, the fans, who are the true gatekeepers of Michael's legacy. It is us who are the heroes.

It is us, Mr. Branca; it is us that are Michael Jackson now.

**

I'll be honest. I still don't think I've properly grieved for Michael. The initial heartbreak reverberated into a militant need to defend him against the soul-parasites leeching off his legacy, which is precisely at the point I remain.

Michael's death broke my heart for two reasons: firstly, with the acknowledgment of the positive qualitative impact that the man indubitably had on my life; and secondly, at the recollection of his life as one that contained such unquenchable sadness – one in which a five year old boy was whipped into shape for our listening pleasure. Why could Michael convey the pain of heartbreak at such a young age? Ask the man stood behind him holding the switch. It was a veritable tragedy of Shakespearean proportions. Michael carried the hopes of his family. He would grow up to take on that mantle for the world; a world that started in the palm of his hand, before eventually becoming the weight on his shoulders.

The June of 2013 was an especially intense one for us fans: a strange song of nostalgia and defiance, with only the heartening bridge of the 13th providing us with brief respite before the emotive crescendo that is the 25th. We followed a similar trajectory in the preparation for the *This Is It* concerts; journeying as we did from the press conference, to the excitement of hearing reports from fans listening to rehearsals, to watching him starve with stress in front of our eyes; fans telling Michael it wasn't worth it; to stop putting himself under all that pressure. As had become the pattern, we accompanied the man on his rise to an angelic apex, before descending alongside him in his fall from grace.

And this time he died.

The AEG Live trial was an attempt by Katherine Jackson and Michael's children to uncover the truth as to why and how this happened. It saw Michael's elderly mother having to once again defend her family from an onslaught of unwarranted abuse. She is a stoic woman. Not only is this a woman who has given birth ten times, she is also someone who has managed to cope with the grief of losing two of these children. It's easy to see where Michael got his gentle leadership attributes and 'rhinoceros skin' from (though I personally prefer the analogy of that other pachyderm, the elephant – I imagine Katherine leading her herd, as they hold each other's tails, yet independently making their own way through life - reconvening on occasion to rejoice or mourn).

But the AEG trial was the first time the eighty-three year old had been in court every day as a plaintiff. The previous occasion in which Katherine had attended court every day was in 2005, as a supporter of her son the defendant: throughout which, she remained composed and gracious in her stolid knowledge of the truth. Yet the salacious details Katherine had to endure through the AEG trial put even the 2005 accusations in the shade. The pornographic details describing her son's physical and mental demise towards death evoked painfully evident tears, both for justice and remorse. Her recounting the moment she learned Michael had died was nothing short of harrowing, "everything went dark, and I just heard screaming."

It was those people with pitiful hearts that believed greed - rather than the anguish and agony of a family who have lost a son and a father - was the motivating factor behind Katherine's mission for justice. Why is it that the Jackson family aren't afforded the same basic level of humanity as others? Why are other families - families that haven't donated sometimes self-sabotaging amounts of money to charity - entitled to the idea of their grief and right to compensation being genuine, whilst the Jacksons aren't? "Never for money, always for love" was a lived philosophy that inspired Michael's often profligate philanthropy, and helped to steep him deep in financial difficulties. Well, that and the way his money was siphoned off by thieves.

Katherine regaled many intimate details to the AEG court - of which, she was the veritable queen - including such anecdotes as the sleeping arrangements of the poverty-stricken *Jackson 5*: a triple bunk bed – Jackie on his own in one, with the other four brothers sharing the other two. (Perhaps Jackie smelled a bit.)

***

The heady days of the confidence of Katherine Jackson's attorney, Brian Panish, and his self-assured arguments for the prosecution seem an age ago. The general fan consensus at the time was of watertight faith in the plaintiff's case; a seeming inevitability that justice would prevail. Karen Faye was the last person standing from Michael's employed inner circle, and there she was taking a stand for the Jackson family in an attempt to get justice for them. The expectation to win was almost palpable; it being practically inconceivable that the Jackson family could lose the trial. The facts, after all, were starkly evident.

However, upon AEG being backed into a corner by the terrible truth, they became a dangerous animal. Although wounded, the company possessed a great deal of power within the media; a power they were not afraid to wield. Thus commenced the first of several smear campaigns, the first one promulgated by AEG-affiliated UK tabloid newspaper, *The Mirror*. The timing of the rehash of twenty-year old allegations was deemed 'suspicious' by Michael's 2005 attorney, Tom Mesereau. AEG stooges had to up the ante in their Public Relations war, hence the front-page tabloid frenzy. Oblivious as usual to fact-checking, and with the requisite attempt at maximum reputation assassination, the truth was that the tapes forming the foundation of this slandering had been discredited ten years ago: to the extent that they were dismissed as useless and baseless by investigators involved in the farcical 2005 trial.

Michael's nephew Taj Jackson filed a claim to the Press Complaints Commission pointing out, point by point, the errors in the story. When the Estate got wind of being beaten to the punch, they, in turn, filed their own complaint to the PCC. As the official point of reference for 'all things Michael Jackson', the Estate's complaint superceded Taj's and was treated as the 'primary' complaint. The result being the sabotage of Taj's initial complaint as - later evidenced on the PCC's public complaints logging system - the Estate neglected to respond to the PCC's follow-up emails.

In a barely-mustered effort to appear neutral, the tabloids then afforded a small article to Prince Jackson's damning eyewitness testimony of AEG's negligence in the care of his father; one that included a mention of his cousin's testimony, incorporating what would normally be the earth-shattering comment that he believed Michael had been murdered. The front pages of that summer's tabloids were a sickening reminder of visits to newsagents in the dark days of 1993, when the slander had been an almost daily occurrence. But Michael's fight to prove his innocence is now too ingrained in the global psyche. He commands too much respect. The rehashed allegations were nothing more than the tactical final death throes of a desperate company, panicking in the process of losing everything to the truth.

Except, of course, they didn't.

In the opening of the AEG case, the defence threatened "we're going to show some ugly stuff." Katherine's lawyer, Mr. Panish asked her, "And how does it make you feel to hear that they're going to tell everyone that your son is a bad person?" To which she replied, "Makes me feel real bad, because I know my son was a very good person. He loved everybody. He gave to charity. He's in the Guinness book of records for giving the most to charity of all the pop stars. I'm so nervous. I'm sorry."

Panish also asked, "And why is it that you're here to testify today?" Katherine replied, "Because I want to know what really happened to my son, and that's why I'm here."

There was a theory that Michael had been dead for hours before Conrad Murray called the paramedics, which is why he was apparently making such a feeble show of performing CPR. This theory arose from the revelation that Michael's skin was cold to the touch when the paramedics arrived, and that his open eyes had had time to dry out.

The AEG trial concluded with the decision that Conrad Murray had been hired by the company as a competent doctor – with him now seeking to retrieve his licence to practice medicine. Whilst also being completely free to cash in on his crime. This is a man who - as part of his defence for killing Michael - spontaneously sprang into the song

'The Little Boy That Santa Claus Forgot'. During an interview on live TV. From jail. In April.

Conrad Murray killed a man who trusted him. A man, who, before being corrupted by ultimately corroborated paranoia, was trusting to a fault.

Murray was sentenced to the statutory maximum of four years imprisonment for involuntary manslaughter, but only served two of these due to a U.S. Supreme Court decision on state prison conditions.

Five fans were subsequently awarded compensation of one euro each in damages from Conrad Murray, as a result of their emotional distress at Michael's death. And although this token payment may seem offensive, the fact that these fans took it as far as they did, and won, is hugely totemic.

However - to utilise Jermaine Jackson's succinct and poetic description - Conrad Murray was merely "the finger to a bigger hand". The production, release and promotion of the video diary of a dying man entitled *This Is It* - in its very essence and existence - lays bare the identities of the more authoritative criminals.

A majority of the jury agreed that AEG Live escaped prosecution on a mere technicality.

Michael Jackson fans have been forced to become activists for justice in the same way Nelson Mandela's supporters had to – a comparison which in no way belittles Nelson Mandela's battle. As Martin Luther King Jr, that other black luminary, once commanded, "Injustice anywhere is a threat to justice everywhere." Indeed, many of Michael's videos are imbued with an undercurrent of activism. Even Michael himself said, "My fans are activists, they will fight you to defend me."

What inspires and consoles me is witnessing the hard work undertaken by so many people in their effort to try and cease this dilution of Michael's life work. And to think how proud of them Michael would be. He would have known that due to the loyalty of his fans, his legacy was in safe hands; in spite of what I'm sure he knew was in store.

MJ's Legacy / heal the world miracle project in Uganda / michael's dream foundation, he left a most concrete and real legacy of goodwill behind him, as evidenced by the Liberia Everland Children's Home project. Haiti. It is projects like these that make me most proud to be a fan of Michael's. Changing the world for the better, one disadvantaged soul at a time.

Michael's commercial resurgence in popularity this time is that it is an artificial one manufactured by the Estate: one focussed on profit rather than the protection and promotion of Michael's art and humanity. It is a false bastardisation worth fighting against. And as

Michael demonstrated, even pacifists can become soldiers when their principles and loves are pushed too far.

Perhaps my defence of Michael is my expression of grief. All I know is - as the years go by, overcast as they are by clouds of continued injustice - the pain remains the same.

CHAPTER SIX

At the apex of the topmost division there stands sometimes only a single man. His joyful vision is like an inner, immeasurable sorrow. Those who are closest to him do not understand him and in their indignation, call him deranged: a phoney or a candidate for the madhouse

KANDINSKY

Michael understood that there is magic in nostalgia; that nostalgia is emotional time-travel; that magic becomes manifest through the mind and its perceptions. And as much as Michael enjoyed entertaining with stage magic (who can forget the introduction to the 1993 *Superbowl* half-time performance – Michael Jackson… somehow in three places at once!), as he expressed in his song 'Mind Is The Magic', the reality is that, "Your own thoughts play the game / In the magical wonders they do / The mind in the magic is you". That is, order and normality is illusory. Michael's very dance was all about the boundaries between reality and illusion – seeming to walk both forwards and backwards at the same time.

And it was this kind of magic - real magic - that Michael wrote about in his book, *Dancing The Dream,* within which he describes magic as being how the thrill that a toddler experiences when watching a tadpole wriggle in mud, is akin to an adult's encounter with the majesty of a whale crashing in the ocean.

As children, we were all alchemists. We combined our ingredients of mud, grass and leaves, and with the mix we made cake. Sometimes I sit down in crowded areas and imagine what the world is like from the perspective of a child - ponder how frightened and vulnerable children must sometimes feel when confronted with the bustle of a busy street, as they're surrounded by strangers two or three times their own size, whilst also marvelling at the courage it entails to engage with this alien world, regardless. It is a courage generated by the same miraculous naivety that makes a child oblivious to their muddied clothes, in spite of their maddened mother - because dirty linen simply pales in pathetic comparison when compared to the majesty of a mud pie.

This was the magic that inspired Michael. When the mystery of the gravity-defying 'Smooth Criminal' lean was made public by the press, Michael responded by wondering why anyone would want to reveal the mechanics that undermined the sense of magic. His desires to prolong childhood and chase dreams were borne of the same principle. Revered movie director John Ford famously said, "If it's a choice between the truth and the legend, print the legend." A sentiment Michael very much agreed with. After all, it was Diana Ross that discovered the *Jackson 5* - right?

Real magic is an encounter with the unfathomable. It transports you back to childhood, when your naiveties expose a vacuum of knowledge concerning how things work. And it was with this kind of heart, this "quality of wonder" – as author Howard Bloom described it, when reflecting upon Michael's life – with which Michael reigned over Neverland. An environment conjured by a musical magician, with its sole raison d'etre of encouraging children to simply enjoy, as Michael called it, "the playfulness of life".

Though the pure enchantment of Neverland also blindsided its unsolicited adult visitors into rediscovering their inner child, too. It was a place where adults could leap over their egos, and emancipate themselves of the constraints of self-consciousness that is the curse of adulthood.

Michael entertained many, many sick and dying children at Neverland, but one child that he became particularly close to and formed a famous friendship with, was Ryan White. Ryan lived with HIV/AIDS for seven years after being diagnosed aged just eleven years old. Ryan and Michael's relationship was instrumental in evolving people's understanding of the disease and helping to diminish the prejudices associated with it.

Another specific child that Michael helped, was the focus of a 2014 fan campaign that flooded Twitter in an attempt to create awareness of Michael's humanitarian efforts. It was the example of Bela Farkas, a four-year-old Hungarian boy who Michael funded the liver transplant for, and hence saved the life of. The reason for the re-emergence of this story was down to the fact that Farkas had recently become a father himself.

***

When I was a little boy, I used to imagine that, living in the attic, was one specimen of every animal that existed on Earth. And on weekday mornings, I would venture up to the attic to choose and retrieve one of these animals to accompany me to school for the day. Typically, I opted for either a tiger, a chimpanzee or an elephant. When I got home, I would return the animal to its menagerie of imaginary friends. Said attic was in my childhood home – the place where I spent the most formative fifteen years of my life. To this day, my sleeping dreams – regardless of the context – are most often played out within the walls of that house.

Michael bought Neverland in 1988, aged thirty years old. He would inhabit it for fifteen years. During which time, it would serve as both his utopia and refuge. It was a place nothing short of outrageous in its pure expression of self and freedom. Truly, Neverland was Michael's soul made manifest. After the 2005 trial, Michael was advised by his legal team that a return to his spiritual home would be foolhardy; a legal team distinctly aware of the ruthlessness of arch-nemesis Tom Sneddon - a man with an insatiable and apparently psychotic vendetta.

Each concert of the *Bad* tour of 1988-89 ended with the words, "Make that change." In 1989, Michael released the 'Leave Me Alone' video, in which he exorcised himself of the materialistic attitude that encapsulated the 1980s (much to his artistic detriment, according to the music critics). Following on from the phenomenon that was the *Bad* project – in particular, 'Man In The Mirror' – Michael attempted to focus his life and career more specifically on humanitarian efforts.

The last time Michael performed every song live on tour was during the first leg of the *Bad* tour. The first leg was essentially a solo interpretation of the *The Jacksons' Victory* tour of 1985. The fluidity of the *Victory* tour dancing – though not as refined as later shows - elicits the same genius and expression of effort that the penultimate phase before the sculptors of the sphinx must have experienced before they decided to stop chiselling. It's all there. But the subsequent tour without the 'shackles' of his brothers is where Michael, inevitably, came into his own. There is a precision, a perfection.

Yet, the first leg is often overlooked due to its bootlegged ubiquity, with fans during the eighties and nineties craving shows from the second leg, what with footage from it being so elusive. This scarcity of footage is a paradox, as the window between the first leg and the second leg appears to be when Michael realised that there was a much bigger job to be done than merely entertaining people. He appreciated his potency, influence and responsibilities. It was a watershed. 'Man In The Mirror' closed the shows, and 'Another Part Of Me' (a lyrical precursor to 'Jam' from the subsequent *Dangerous* album) was incorporated into the set, with Michael changing the adlib from the record, "This is our doom" to "This is my plan."

After kicking off the first leg of the world tour in Japan, Michael returned there for the second leg, with his new-found message. Subsequent to the commercial successes of the eighties and nineties, Michael would persist in insisting that "The best is yet to come". A statement ridiculed by many – yet, who is to say that Michael was referencing his art? It seems far more plausible - considering his eternally untouchable artistic successes; his donning of the mantle of most famous person on the planet, and his voluntary assumption of using this status as a conduit for goodwill - that Michael was alluding to his humanitarian work. As he said, "In the 1990's, I will promise you the best work I've ever done. Always help the children, love them."

Neverland became a custom-made physical construct of this mentality. Michael's exploitation of the rampant capitalism that defined the eighties made the development of Neverland a fiscal possibility – but once this had been accomplished, Michael transformed his home into something of substance and importance.

He elevated Neverland into "a place called Hallowed Ground" – Michael wrote 'Speechless' whilst watching children play there.

Neverland was an oasis of solace and innocence. Like the protagonist in Salvador Dali's painting *Female Figure with Head of Flowers*, Neverland shone as a beacon of beauty in an otherwise-arid landscape bedevilled by searching, solitude, regret and servitude: both metaphorically-speaking, and physically. The racketeering attempt of 2005 struck at the very core of his philosophy; his mission; his heart. It tore off the petals and trampled them into the oblivion of the surrounding dust.

The bustling laughter of children gives anywhere an inherent sense of unbridled joy. The playground that was Neverland became ghostly silent in its grief for those children that fell victim to the demonic personalities infected by "the same disease of lust, gluttony and greed", as Michael laments in the *HIStory* album track, 'Money'. The actions of a pitifully envious few, hell-bent on monetary gain, were the ones that raped children. Not Michael.

***

I was recently watching my two young daughters run around the local park. They approached people without prejudice, their curiosity craving the sating of a question on their minds: "Why is your baby crying?" or "Can you ride a bicycle, too?" They indiscriminately engage with strangers, usually introducing themselves with the ostensibly random knowledge of how old they are. They are an unparalleled pleasure to observe. Yet, there was something in their demeanour that reminded me of the horrors I have personally witnessed on the streets of the Kenyan capital of Nairobi. The thirst for knowledge that I recognised in my children's faces caused me to recall the look in the eyes of Kenyan children of a similar age – pre-schoolers – who begged for money from people passing by: money that would be spent on the drugs to which they had become addicted; drugs that helped them escape the reality of their tragic situation.

I recently happened upon an interview with the actor Zac Efron (as one does.) In it, Mr. Efron describes – as a fortuitous consequence of working with Kenny Ortega on the *High School Musical* movie franchise – how he was handed a phone on which Michael was on the other end. Zac Efron is a lifelong fan of Michael's, and the surprise that was his being on the phone to his idol, resulted in him breaking down in uncontrollable tears. Unable to compose himself, Zac handed the phone back to Kenny Ortega, who ended the call. Michael then phoned back and asked to speak to the actor. Michael was also now crying. Through the mutual sobs, Michael managed to utter the words, "See? Dreams do come true."

I believe that Michael was weeping in the piqued hope of believing his own dreams would one day come to fruition: that all his efforts in forging a cultural foundation upon a belief in the wisdom of childhood would one day be realised; that all the sacrifice will have been worth it. After all – and with total respect to the likeable man – I somehow doubt Michael was plaintive at the realisation of a dream involving talking to Zac Efron on the phone.

The proposed sale of Neverland by the Estate – the physical construct, remember, that inimitably expresses Michael's soul – is a tragedy. Michael acquiesced to participate in *This Is It* for financial reasons, though at the same time persevering in earnestly dismissing the idea of selling Neverland (or his unpublished music, for that matter).

In 2003, Michael said,

"I wanted to have a place where I could create everything I never had as a child... I love it. And I will always love it. And I will never, ever sell Neverland. Neverland is me... You know? It represents the totality of who I am. It really does... I love Neverland."

In 2012, a legal spokesperson for Katherine Jackson said, "It is the wish of the beneficiaries that Neverland be kept in the family, and Michael's children one day decide what to do with their home." In 2013, Paris Jackson spoke about her wish to return and resurrect this childhood home. In a few mere years, Michael's children will gain personal control of their inherited share of their father's multi-millions (should they still exist). Why can't the lawyers at the helm of the Estate of Michael Jackson fund the preservation of this culturally-precious, historically-significant and much-cherished childhood home until then? The place where Michael's children grew up not having to imagine retrieving animals from their attic, as those very real animals lived in their garden? Animals that lived there because Michael so clearly and inherently understood the idiosyncratic yearnings of youth.

Legal advice or otherwise, it is no wonder that Michael never returned to Neverland. Instead, he embarked on a world tour of an altogether different ilk – he became nomadic, traversing the globe looking for somewhere that he could settle with his children, unworried and secure.

Michael craved privacy. He understood that privacy is crucial for potential; for creativity; for democracy. Another example of his dichotomous nature was his being the most recognisable person on the planet, yet also the most private. His philosophy made concrete, that to be truly free, one must exist within an environment that allows the flourishing of an individual's potential, in order to be able to contribute wholly to society.

Michael argued that it should be possible to have a celebrity's relationship with the media, as well as a private one: that the two were mutually exclusive. In the 1997 Barbara Walters interview, Michael argues there is a time and a place for paparazzi involvement – fully acknowledging that it's part and parcel of the game of self-promotion, but simultaneously suggesting that there is a cut-off point (perhaps just before hiding cameras in toilets whilst simultaneously taking photographs from helicopters flying overhead?). Michael said,

"There should be some boundaries, the star needs some space. He has a heart... he is human."

Whilst wandering the world, Michael continued to love artistry; continued to lift his head from the drowning waters of attempted oppression and make his voice heard. Or - as he put it in 'Unbreakable' - "steady laughin' while surfacin'." Michael never stopped writing, even whilst in exile: songs such as 'People of the World' and 'Days in Gloucestershire' - the latter example evoking an image of a man in peaceful and deserved semi-retirement, lazily picking at grass whilst lying in a field blessed in sunshine. There is a real, simple beauty to it. 'People of the World' demonstrates that Michael's determination to unite the world through melody was unrelenting.

But above his craft and all, Michael's love was for his children. As he sang himself, his children were his life. There's a reason Michael had less time for his artistry in his final decade on Earth: he was a hands-on single father.

As I have mentioned, I also have the honour of being a father. Something that involves the divine privilege of listening to a four year old and a two year old serenade me with adaptations of *Jackson 5* songs that are somewhat less-than-faithful to the originals. Though my children possess quite different musical tastes: whereas the elder daughter likes to pirouette and float gracefully to ballads, the younger likes to head-bounce to funk. The younger's favourite *Jackson 5* song is 'Dancing Machine' (at the drop of the tune, she comes alive), whereas this fondness for 'Dancing Machine' is ridiculed by my elder daughter for her belief in the song containing the lyric, "croc-oc-odile" (it doesn't, of course – but if you listen to the refrain "Watch her get down", you can tell exactly what she means). The elder's favourite is 'I'll Be There'. Or, as she croons it, "I'm A Bear". Running around in circles with the single-minded determination of catching up with themselves is a dance move they can both agree on, however. And the one song they have a mutual appreciation for is 'ABC'.

Yeah. It's on a lot that one.

Indeed, perhaps the only song I've sang on more occasions in my life than 'Billie Jean', is 'Twinkle, Twinkle Little Star'. During those long, long nights of settling babies down to sleep.

Now. Imagine if someone threatened to take them away from me?

There were cries for Michael to have his children taken away from him after the second wave of allegations.

Imagine what that would have done to him?

***

The talent and genius of Michael Jackson almost becomes redundant in the face of what he tried to utilise the resulting fame for – an attempt at a legacy that makes the world a better place, beginning with a universal reverence for childhood. Michael gathered the waifs and strays - the lost children - and led them to a land of pure escapism. Not only in the physical snapshot of eternal youth that was Neverland, but on a much larger scale, through his art and his mantra of following one's dreams.

Michael never won the Nobel Peace Prize, although he was twice nominated - in 1998 and 2003 - and was surely the most worthy human being to have never acquired it. Nevertheless, in spite of this particular accolade not having adorned any of the many mantelpieces of Neverland, Michael did receive some twenty internationally-recognised humanitarian awards, as well as countless other recognitions and tributes, including a *Guinness Book of World Records* entry for the *Most Charities Supported By A Pop Star* (thirty-nine), and an eponymous music industry award that continues to be annually presented in celebration of that year's most philanthropic musical artist. As well as this, Michael set up his own charity, the *Heal The World Foundation*, for which he toured the world to raise funds – donating every penny of the proceeds from it - before having the charity deliver aid by military planes to the innocent people caught up in the war in Sarajevo. All this, before even mentioning his constant striving to use his talent and status to release globally-recognisable musical anthems bearing the sole purpose of inspiring peace and unity amongst the human race.

As the Icelandic musician Bjork surmised, "[Michael's] religion is 'magic' and he has a fanatical belief in hope and that everything is going to be alright."

Michael's self-imposed exile in Neverland was due to the sense of incongruity he felt with the cynicism of the adult world. He wanted to disassociate himself from a corrupted system. The turbulence and brutality of the world and its media empires that were prejudiced against him, meant Neverland was the place where Michael sought refuge. As he said,

"People become addicted to the world and the violence. And they become subjected to other people's thoughts and to the American system. Our way is not the only way."

To illustrate this point, there's a humorous example in which Michael, at the conclusion to a commercial for *Suzuki*, turns to the camera and appears to attempt to wink, but blinks instead. Of course, we see in the 'Smooth Criminal' video, that Michael is more than capable of winking. In Japan, however, where the advert was shown, blinking means 'love'.

Michael built Neverland with the sole purpose of creating a haven for the celebration of childhood - as a retreat for an unhindered exploration of the purity and potential of youth; as somewhere he could escape the societal 'norms' thrust – unsolicited – upon us all. 'Norms' that consistently attempt to corrupt the very concept of love, in any of its given forms. 'Tarantism' is the word given to describe the act of banishing melancholy through the act of dancing. It was the refuge of Neverland that provided Michael with the solitude and privacy to "escape the world" and "enjoy that simple dance." Before it was ransacked in 2005, whereupon Michael's utopian pocket of eternal youth was irreparably corrupted by the monstrous ugliness of a perverted and emotionally retarded outside world.

In *Moonwalker*, Michael had an actor playing a young version of himself perform a skit of his 'Bad' video. The actor then transforms into the adult Michael. The peculiarity of Michael's friends dressing up as him is often seized upon by critics. The reason for this could be as prosaic as his friends merely wanting to dress as their hero (after all, thousands of people do this without even having met Michael). Or maybe it was an attempt by Michael to marry his pre-*Thriller* persona with his post-*Thriller* self.

Neverland was not a paedophile's lure; it was a true expression of innocence. The problem wasn't Michael's perspective, it was theirs. It was the rest of the world that needed to recover their inner child, not Michael. People query Michael's choice to spend his time in the company of children, without ever questioning the reason why millions of people sought to seek his presence when he was a child. As well as whilst he remained childlike as an adult. Michael saw more individual human beings than anyone else that has ever existed. Because they flocked in their hundreds of millions to go and see him.

Adorning one wall of Michael's bedroom at Neverland was a framed picture of Jesus Christ, which was surrounded by pictures of *Disney* characters; his house was inhabited by statues and mannequins of cartoon figures. Though Michael's fashion was lavish and iconic when in the public eye, the wardrobes of his bedroom were filled with red shirts and white T-shirts, which when at home, he wore every day.

Michael was uniquely complicated. We are not expected to fully understand. But, as civilised human beings, we are expected to infer positivity from his experience, as part of an endeavour to transform the world for the better.

For everyone.

The alternative is outright disaster.

People believe what they need to believe. The world needs to believe in the integrity of Michael Jackson's message of innocence.

CHAPTER SEVEN

Every child that is born is proof that God has not yet given up on human beings.

RABINDRANATH TAGORE

The sun takes twelve days to set after its glorious zenith on what fans now refer to as *Vindication Day*. During these twelve days, clouds gradually gather: tinged by the touch of the star's tragic tiring - exacerbating an increasing anxiety that ultimately succumbs to the bleak and black sadness that is the anniversary of Michael's death.

Children were simultaneously Michael's Achilles' heel and his vitality. His single-mindedness in being their advocate was his only vulnerability; a pressure point that was exploited with aplomb. As Michael said, "They try to use my love for children against me and it's so unfair, I'm very upset about it you know?"

Michael's artistic riposte to the 1993 extortion attempt is dedicated to all the children of the world, who he claims responsibility for. Michael loved all children the way any mother loves their own.

There comes a time in most people's lives when the fig leaf falls and the Eden of childhood ceases to be. What with the lifelong constancy of Michael's childhood, there were inevitably various occasions when the fig leaves of his fans fell, whilst his remained. Michael's work being categorised into eras provides a convenient system for measuring this.

The first instance of such corruption was with the release of *Dangerous* in 1991. Grunge was the coming-of-age rally cry for the turn-of-the-decade teenager, and Nirvana's *Nevermind* album stole the cool vote. Michael had anticipated the change in mood and 'Give In To Me' - which had initially been mooted as a dance number - became Michael's rock response.

The contradiction is that *Dangerous* is often described as Michael's coming-of-age album. Yet, as he concocted a different image for each era, a case can be made for all of them: *Off The Wall* – his first solo album featuring self-penned material, a falsetto exhale that embodied the entire genre of disco; *Thriller* – the historic unit-and-culture shifting phenomenon; *Bad* – all songs bar two self-penned, as well as his first tour as a solo performer; *HIStory* – a unique polemic sparked by a very unique inspirational spur; *Invincible* – his desire to be emancipated from Sony Music.

Though remaining stolid throughout all these distinct phases, was Michael continuing to be childlike.

The evidence for which, is ubiquitously extant: the sincere glee in Michael's laughter during the custard-pie fight shown in the making of 'Black Or White'; the genuine giddiness in the film of Michael and Macaulay Culkin dropping water bombs on people brave enough to pass beneath their hotel balcony; the palpability of the incredulity in Michael's voice when asking the smiling executioner Martin Bashir, "You don't climb trees?.. You missing out…" the delirious delight emanating from a man in his thirties charging around in a dodgem whilst eating candy floss.

Commentators of a certain ilk often remark and opine with pop-insight that a lot of Michael's problems could have been resolved by a good therapist; how his yearning for his lost childhood could have been sated by some time spent embracing his inner child. In reality, a therapist sitting opposite Michael, attempting to help him harmonise with his inner child, would have had to contend with a man daydreaming about how to best employ his next practical joke. Michael spent each and every day embracing his inner child: meeting him at the door; welcoming him with reconciliation and rejoicing. He celebrated childhood daily – both its innocence and mischief.

Michael's predilection for "such elementary things" as he describes in the *HIStory* track, 'Childhood', is evident in his words,

"I feel that they are more than just children; that they are all little geniuses and that they have a secret all of their own. A secret that they cannot always express. [...] I studied child psychology because of my love for children – all over the world. [...] If a kid doesn't like you, he'll tell you. But adults pretend and put on phoney ways. I wish the world could be full of children!"

Though this revering of naivety is by no means peculiar to him; indeed it is a trait commonly found in adults who have suffered unorthodox upbringings.

Brian Wilson, the troubled chief songwriter for the *Beach Boys*, is another example of a childlike musical luminary fond of activities that most people would deem to be unusual.

During his youth, Wilson experienced such horrors at the hands of his ferocious father as the macabre punishment of being forced to stare into his father's empty eye socket. When terrors such as this are inflicted on the mutable and sensitive mind of a child, the resultant eccentricities in their adult behaviour suddenly become much more comprehensible. Consoling themselves by indulging in idiosyncrasies with which they feel affinity, is the right of these individuals - not merely as human beings, but also, in the case of such people as Michael and Wilson, in their status as agents of priceless artistic pulchritude with which they illuminate humanity.

In Wilson's case, behaviours that would ostensibly be seen as bizarre by a prejudging public, include a sincere love for the US TV series about a heroic dolphin named Flipper – at which he would often cry; and his keeping of a menagerie of mechanical pets.

The essence of Michael's philosophy is that a man such as Wilson's father can only have become so cruel as a consequence of himself having suffered an abusive childhood. The term 'abuse', however, is vague and envelops a wide spectrum. What one child interprets as abuse may be very different to how another experiences it. After all, there were five members of the *Jackson 5*, yet none of them were as traumatised by the experience as much as Michael was. Which is why Michael's philosophy was more concerned with pinpointing specific needs when helping to realise the potential of an individual.

In the lyrics for the *Thriller* album outtake, 'Scared of the Moon', Michael laments the repercussions of negative childhood experiences,

"The years go by swiftly /And soon childhood ends / But life is still fearful / When evening descends / But now there are others who sit in their room / And wait for the sunlight to brighten their gloom /

Together they gather / Their lunacy shared / Not knowing just why they're scared / Scared of the moon".

***

Michael said - with utmost sincerity – that he was "Peter Pan in his heart."

Michael was a famously voracious reader, and within his vast library existed a number of J.M Barrie biographies. Michael evidently found affinity with the life story of the author of *Peter Pan.* The vast vacuum of self that resulted from such a uniquely peculiar upbringing as Michael's became filled with the story of Barrie, his artistry, and the love he received from his fans, and later, children. The love his children provided is perhaps another reason why Michael rarely took to the stage during the latter decade of his life.

Michael's gravitation towards the Peter Pan personality coincided chronologically with the self-motivation note he wrote to himself in which he decided to become a whole other person. Of course, this also coincided with Michael growing physically into an adult man. Perhaps this choice to inhabit Peter Pan was a subconscious longing to keep hold of the love he had experienced from the public as a child? The only love, apart from his mother, that he'd ever experienced.

Concurrently, this Peter Pan persona also contained the side-effect of being enigmatic – and gave him the option of testing conformity. It could also have been a subconscious attempt at self-sabotage, or a test of the loyalty of those around him.

In the footage of Michael eating candy floss in the dodgem, he is wearing one of the jackets used for 'Jam' on the *Dangerous* tour. The image is a fascinating juxtaposition that demonstrates the dichotomy between Michael the man-boy and Michael the man-performer.

This capacity for transformation can be seen during the Wembley *Bad* tour rendition of 'Dirty Diana'. Watch - after a hunched, self-conscious walk through the dark towards centre-stage - how Michael spontaneously ignites into character with the activation of the spotlight as the first chord is struck. A particular persona possesses him.

Michael didn't live long enough to fulfil his dream of becoming a movie star, what with each of his attempted excursions into the medium seemingly stymied in some way or another (the closest Michael got was with his insistence on referring to his music videos as 'short films', and - although was once nominated for an Academy

Award, which he didn't win - he did buy one in 1999 for a record $1.54 million).

However, one need only to recognise how easily they are moved by any of the many characters he embodied in his plethora of music videos to appreciate that Michael possessed and exuded the requisite charisma to be successful on celluloid. Furthermore, regardless of Michael's lack of movie roles, one only needs to listen to his ability to evoke character through the power of his voice. As Michael said himself in his book, *Dancing The Dream,* "In infinite expressions I come and go." Michael was a great friend of the genius actor Marlon Brando – Brando's final role before his death being his cameo in the 'You Rock My World' video. Brando provided Michael with acting lessons, perhaps in gratitude - what with Brando's self-confessed preferred method for getting into shape for a movie role being to close the living room curtains and dance to Michael's music.

Another entertainment figure that most wouldn't imagine had a great deal in common with Michael, is Lou Reed - what with the differences in their respective artistic output. However, there is honour and understanding among artists, and there is an anecdote in which Reed becomes an unlikely defender of Michael.

The former Czech President, Václav Havel, had hosted Michael in Prague Castle during Michael's stay in the Czech capital on the *HIStory* Tour, in 1996. Nine years later, during the 2005 trial, Havel and Lou Reed, who were great friends, conducted an onstage conversation at Prague's Švandovo divadlo drama theatre. They only disagreed once all evening, and it was over Michael.

Havel had invited Michael to stay with him in 1996, because he was interested in him as a "civilisation phenomenon." However, Havel moaned to the theatre audience that - instead of spending time with him discussing his cultural significance - Michael preferred to "go to the third courtyard and say hello to the children." The audience laughed at Havel's snide and insinuating dig at Michael. However, Lou Reed, annoyed at the audience's reaction, then jumped to Michael's defence, saying, "He's a great singer, a great dancer, then there's all this other stuff and people don't pay attention… I think Michael Jackson is one of the greatest dancers in the world … the Fred Astaire of our generation."

"I recognise his skills, but I'm not a fan," Havel responded.

"He wasn't in my castle," retorted Reed, eliciting a far bigger laugh than Havel had managed to muster with his lazy cynicism.

Havel had hosted Michael, then harboured his bullying anecdote for nine years before this event. It took a creative and non-judgmental mind such as Lou Reed's to see beyond the painfully superficial perspective of the Czech President. It's yet another example of treating Michael as a pariah because of his differences; of cynics abusing their positions and Michael's vulnerabilities to intensify his insecurities for their own gain; of referring to encounters with him as "meeting the freak," as the slavish, fat cat employers referred to their starving and emaciated employee (another of the insults revealed for all to see in the email correspondence produced as evidence in the AEG trial). Their employee – a man that co-owned the most valuable music catalogue on the planet, who was now somehow in a position in which he was frantically desperate to be capable of earning enough money to put a roof over his children's heads. A man that was doing this by spreading his message; a message that demanded the world prioritise a universal love and respect for children and childhood.

During 'I'll Be There', over decades of performing it live, Michael was the man that cried nightly tears in front of millions and millions of people - tears pricked, he conceded, as a consequence of being overwhelmed by thoughts of the plight of suffering children. 'I'll Be There' is an anthem for the bereft – for anyone plaintive for anyone missed. It is just one of the three concert mainstays that survived the forty years since the *Jackson 5* era, and the only one given the honour of being played at full-length. The sentiment it carries of erstwhile or elsewhere loved ones nevertheless being present wherever love is found, is a powerful and healing one.

Due to its presence on a posthumous poster, there is one quote from Michael that has become particularly prominent. It encapsulates his philosophy, one borne of hard-earned wisdom,

"If you enter this world knowing you are loved and you leave this world knowing the same, then everything that happens in between can be dealt with."

This common-sense creed formed the crux of the theme of his speech at the 2001 Oxford Address, which Michael gave to promote his *Heal The Kids* initiative,

"Friends, the foundation of all human knowledge, the beginning of human consciousness must be that each and every one of us is an object of love… before you know if you have red hair or brown… before you know if you are black or white… before you know what religion you are a part of… you have to know that you are loved."

Michael was the man that, after seeing starving children on television, wrote 'Be Not Always', with its lyrics, "Faces - did you see their faces? / Did they touch you? / Have you felt such pain?" Before then organising, writing and recording the biggest selling charity single of all time, in an effort to fund aid for these faces. He was the man that dedicated his *Bad* tour Yokohama performance of 'I Just Can't Stop Loving You' to the murdered boy, Yoshiaki Hagiwara. Michael was the man who, suffocating in an opiate-driven oblivion towards the end of his life, remained adamant in his intention to build the world's biggest children's hospital.

Childhood is a period of utopia perpetually repeated for all time, just by differing people. It is a phase of existence content in its inherent disregard of the differences between people, even that of language. This utopia is what people attempt to recreate through the retrograde reach that is the recreational use of opiate drugs. Michael included.

In the lyrics to 'A Place With No Name', Michael sings about finding what he "can fix", before discovering a "place where no people have pain" in which "kids are playin'... and no-one's in fear." The broken-down car depicted in 'A Place With No Name' is a far cry from the funk vehicle imagined in 1987's 'Speed Demon', in which Michael sings, "Speed Demon, you're the very same one who said the future's in your hands, the life you save could be your own."

It is nothing less than a criminal tragedy that Michael was coerced into such extremes of escapism as opiate abuse – primarily as a consequence of the spiritual pillaging wreaked upon his home and solace, Neverland.

Michael was, of course, in many ways an enigma. But the beauty of an enigma is in its openness to interpretation: if no-one knows the secret, it becomes a mirror; a reflection of the perceiver's desires. Construing Michael is akin to assembling a huge jigsaw whilst holding a limited amount of pieces. It's your own perception that completes the image. Except, with our enigma, we also had evidence.

Evidence that he was generous to a fault, and obsessed with the notion of using his fame to promote a message of peace.

Michael was both as emotionally charged, yet as carefully crafted as a poem. He was the puppet Pinocchio that eventually realised his dream of becoming a flesh-and-bone human boy. He was the lonely man paradoxically cheered by billions. The only time Michael wasn't alone was when he was in the company of those people he trusted: children of his age - people on the cusp of pubescence – merely three of whom, out of the thousands that visited Neverland, became corrupted by the greed of adults, and abetted his betrayal. It was hardly surprising Michael was wary of adults, though nevertheless, time after time one hears recollections of visitors to Neverland that recall Michael's parting words being, "come back any time." He was a desperately lonely man caught in the purgatory of public perception. It's a cruel world-view that denies another person like-minded friends. Inhumane, in fact.

No-one is suggesting that there wasn't something unique about Michael's relationship with children. But in lieu of any evidence of wrongdoing, a person's perspective on Michael is entirely a reflection of what the observer wants to see. Perception is a reflection. Baseless hate or unfounded nastiness is merely a projection of one's own insecurity. And in the absence of one shred; one atom; one iota of evidence - in spite of the rape of Neverland, and in the unanimous affirmation of his innocence by a jury - there is not a single reason to suspect Michael as having been anything other than a naive and lonely man taken advantage of by greed. Unless that is what you perversely choose to believe. Michael was the Rorschach Test personified. Any paedophilic monster construed can only be one purposefully selected by an observer actively opting to be ignorant of an indisputable fact - a fact forever petrified into history - that through the outcome of a trial that ultimately killed him, Michael's personal ideology was completely vindicated. He was entirely absolved of any wrongdoing whatsoever concerning illegal behaviour involving children.

Other than Karen Faye, perhaps the other colleague Michael spent most of his time with was his vocal trainer, Seth Riggs, who said,

"I spent thirty-two years with Michael...I vocalised him two hours a day, six days a week. Number one - he was a very sweet man, he was an honest man, and he was not the kind of man who would molest children. That I can promise you. But he loved everyone and he really in many ways spent a lot of money to help other people in need. And I watched him do it. Time after time - again, people that needed help desperately. And who would show up? Michael, with his cheque book. Nobody knows that, they only think about the crazy things that would cause some sort of sensation. But Michael had a heart of gold."

Michael had the financial freedom to revisit the "lost and found" of his childhood on an unprecedented scale: an eccentricity that was seized upon by a cynical society. Yet, most people 'infantilise' themselves to a certain extent – and in the same way Michael noted the hypocrisy of the universal acceptance of Caucasian attempts to change their skin colour to fit in with societal aspirations, it should further be noted how the infantilisation of adults is also done on a mass daily basis for similar reasons. Clothes departments of supermarkets, for example, are stocked to the brim with adult nightwear adorned with images of *Disney* characters: a chance for people to buy into rose-tinted nostalgia, in an attempt to temporarily export themselves back to a time and place where they possessed a kingdom of imagination within which they could find refuge. The commodification and sexualisation of nostalgia is the cynical prostitution of beautiful efforts borne by the fundamental innocence of humanity. (Nostalgia is big business – just ask the Estate.)

Michael fell victim to his naivety of the perception of his philosophies by the outside world. Michael indicated jealousy as a premium motivational reason for acts of 'evil'. Jealous people - people unable to comprehend that sometimes the view of the mountain itself is as beautiful as the view from its summit. Indeed, one may very well argue that the very existence of the mass misunderstanding of Michael's ideology, is due to a deep-seated envy of his precious capacity for being able to see through the eyes of a child; and of his capability to harness this gift for his art and success.

Or perhaps – as demonstrated by those in charge at AEG Live during their ultimately lethal whipping of Michael to perform for *This Is It* – it is that when a majority are hell-bent on getting what they desire, mass psychopathy ensues, and Lord help anyone standing in their way. The global media opprobrium heaped upon Michael during and since the molestation allegations is further testament to this phenomenon. Bringing Michael down sold newspapers – and to hell with the effect such treacherous slander might have on such a sensitive soul.

Two examples of Michael's imploring the world to see his perspective on his associating with children can be found on the *Invincible* album. One of these is in 'The Lost Children' – a cry for everyone to try and rediscover their inner child – where he sings, "I see the door simply wide open / Where no-one can find me," and another in 'Speechless'- a song written whilst watching children at play – in which Michael croons, "When I'm with you I am in the light / Where I cannot be found."

People are extra-performative with those they trust. With their children, especially. Michael had voluntarily adopted the mantle as the father of all the world's children – both those of a young chronological age, and those adults – the "lost" ones – who are so often the people that remain devoted to his mission. Those people that in front of whom, he could perform without the worry of them being prejudice: the ones he surrounded himself with. Michael understood that children innately amplify experiences – of fear; of rage; of the messages contained within a concert; of love. And he lived and breathed this knowledge, along with the responsibility of it, as he delivered his message.

Michael's efforts to maintain his natural character were under perpetual bombardment from those who simply did not possess either the intellectual or emotional capacity to understand him. These attacks – like a storm battering a rock - inevitably, as they would anyone, weathered him. The spray that spat from the media tempest inflicted pain like water torture. Yet regardless, he strived to preserve and express that congenital core of purity.

And this 'weathering' is not merely a metaphor – the attacks physically shaped him. It was this bullying that initially motivated the plastic surgery Michael would ultimately become a poster boy for. Ironically – though very much in keeping with the idea of the entity Michael being a microcosm of the entirety of humanity – plastic surgery has now become an accepted daily feature of our postmodern world. As the man himself said, "plastic surgery wasn't invented for Michael Jackson" – and the sheer hypocrisy of - not only his peers in that Mecca of perceived self-rectification known as Hollywood - but also of any single person that endeavours to artificially alter their appearance to assuage their insecurities: be that breast implantation, teeth-whitening or photoshopped pictures – proves him absolutely right.

Children are oblivious to such superficiality. It is no wonder Michael chose to be around them. Yet, with the befriending of children came a different sadness. The vast majority of these friendships were doomed from the outset to be fleeting. The lyrics detailing the tragedy of the protagonist of the song 'Puff The Magic Dragon' remind me a great deal of Michael – a figure of legend entrapped eternally in a world where friends come and go, as their finite time in the kingdom of childhood comes to an end:

"Dragons live forever but not so little boys / Painted wings and giant strings make way for other toys… / Without his lifelong friend, Puff could not be brave / So Puff that mighty dragon sadly slipped into his cave."

Michael wanted us all to live in his place, one where the platonic companionship of children is an intrinsically acceptable norm. And as Steven Spielberg said, "I wish we could all spend some time in his world."

***

Love is so easily plundered by cynics. There are even certain parts of the USA, where one may openly carry a firearm, yet are denied the option of purchasing a sex toy without possessing a medical prescription – it is the pathologisation and legislation of the simple and most natural act of making love, whilst the promotion of indifference to potential grievous violence continues unchecked. Yet, love is the very reason why, in spite all of humanity's suffering, it persists. Love reigns over pain.

Michael strived to convey a message of anti-violence. He was the Martin Luther King of his generation. He utilised his prominent position on the public pedestal to try and educate against the use of violence, including during acts of protest. After 1993, Michael was placed in, what – for most people – would have been an impossible professional and personal position to return from. Michael responded to this attempted character assassination of him by releasing a song pleading with the people of the Earth to awaken to the damage being done to their planet – a song in which the accompanying short film shows the detonation of an apocalyptic bomb as a little girl runs for her bicycle. These are the wrongdoings that Michael wanted to address – by ensuring that all children were given the ironclad right to a childhood free from abuse, and thus in time ending the cycle. It is the next step in the civilisation of humankind, and history will hold Michael aloft as an evolutionary visionary.

Michael's stance on the wisdom of children is often lazily dismissed. Perhaps because people find it too vague to understand. In truth, however, it is very specific and very simple. By 'being like the children', Michael was suggesting we learn from their innate obliviousness to traits such as race, class or gender: that traits trained into people as they become older, embittered and prejudiced, are nonexistent in children. Children simply request that their innate love for everything is reciprocated. Michael's message was that, regardless of any oppression we might meet, having the wisdom to approach problems with the flexibility of thought of a child is the key to overcoming it.

This is how Michael was like the children. His physicality embodied the differing traits, whilst his philosophy merely asked that the boundless love he possessed for all the people of the planet be reflected back upon him. And he wanted that for everyone. Michael looked at people and saw them as children, and loved them as their mothers did. As he wrote, "Children show me in their playful smiles the divine in everyone. This simple goodness shines straight from their hearts and only asks to be loved."

Michael was the natural antidote to a world that cynically exploits nostalgia and youth.

***

What with his having been the most famous man on the planet, the ripples of Michael's crash-landing on Earth over fifty-five years ago continue to ruffle the leaves and pique the libido of tabloid media editors worldwide, and will long persist in doing so. Just as a murder of media crows circled our martyred Michael whilst he lay on his deathbed in hospital, so they continue to do so now - perched like vultures around their tabloid junkyard, perpetually alert to the possibility of picking at any scraps thrown from a carcass being ravaged by shameless opportunists. To whom, it has suddenly dawned upon, that work opportunities have dried up, and financing the upbringing of their own children - who have become accustomed to a particular standard of living - is going to prove expensive. Now that Michael is dead, these parasites feel no guilt in cashing in on their friendship with him, regardless of whatever nefarious means they are forced to employ. In the process, they put Michael's children through hell.

All of us.

These perennial reappearances to the forefront of the public eye returned once again in the 2014 historical allegations of anal rape. These accusations took us to a hitherto unmentioned level of bestiality, beyond the allegations of mutual masturbation and plying of alcohol to minors. The ante was upped because those previous 'lesser' accusations were discredited in a court of law. The maids quoted by tabloids in an attempt to lend credence to the stories had already been dismissed off-hand by the 2005 jury as "liars". The loaded terminology of 'anal rape' was specifically chosen to leave an indelible smear on the psyche of those that heard it. Similarly, as a riposte to the debacle that was the 2003 *Living With Michael Jackson* documentary, Michael distributed his own version of the interviews entitled *Take 2*. Michael had wisely recorded himself being recorded by Martin Bashir and his team. In *Take* 2, Bashir's unethical techniques of sycophancy and bullying, combined with clever editing, were exposed. However, in a world of press 'exclusives', the damage had already been done.

Towards the end of the Bashir documentary, when asked why the welfare of children meant so much to him, choking back heartfelt tears, Michael responded with the words, "I'm just very sensitive to their pain." Given a platform to speak at Oxford University, Michael used the occasion to propose a Children's Bill of Rights, with one of these being "the right to be loved without having to earn it". Michael promoted these beliefs until his dying breath, as evidenced in the gut-wrenching recording that Conrad Murray made of Michael as he groaned in anaesthetised oblivion, where he is heard talking about his dreams of building a children's hospital. Indeed, the last performance Michael ever made was of 'Earth Song' – in a rehearsal the day before he died – meaning that some of his final utterances on stage were, "What about children dying? / Can't you hear them cry?"

To promote a universal freedom of opportunity for children to fulfil their potential is surely a faultless philosophy, with perhaps the only drawback being its vulnerability to abuse by the laziness of cynicism. Cynicism such as the absurdity contained with the racism charges against Michael – one of the United College Negro College Funds all-time largest contributors. Michael made his reasons for supporting the cause very clear during a speech in 1988 after collecting his honorary doctorate degree of Humane Letters from Fisk University in New York City,

"There is nothing more important than ensuring that everyone has the opportunity to an education. To want to learn, to have the capacity learn but not to be able to is a tragedy."

When conspired against and confronted with the most expensive attempted character assassination in history, remained dignified, before defending himself by utilising his art: a slice of art that attempted to elicit action for change. The *HIStory* project was an uncharacteristically angry sting from Michael. Yet as cathartic as the work must have been for him - like a normally peaceable bee stinging out of terror - it also commenced the process of ripping out his heart. The eventual trial of 2005 tore it out completely.

And his death orphaned us all.

Human nature is self-sabotaging. And of all the dichotomies involving Michael, perhaps the most poignant is how a man that strived so tirelessly through his creativity to make the world a better place, became the man the world strived so hard to destroy. But Michael was appealing to a consciousness beyond the current human state.

***

Whilst unconscious under the effects of Propofol (the anaesthetic Michael turned to after becoming a chronic insomniac – a side-effect of Demerol abuse), no dreaming occurs. It is a tragic irony that Michael - a man synonymous with the power of dreams – in an effort to be physically capable of performing on stage, became the only human being to have ever gone sixty days without actually dreaming.

However, it's too easy to focus on the tragic aspects of Michael's existence. Besides, however much Michael's life became a quagmire, it was ultimately about spreading joy.

Michael divulged that hide-and-seek was one of his favourite games to play. He references it in his poem, *Are You Listening?*

"In infinite expressions I come and go / Playing hide-and-seek / In the twinkling of an eye / But immortality's my game."

The mention of immortality is an important one. Michael's fuel for his success was a faith in its resultant fame being able to influence society's perspective on the role of children in humanity's progression. Michael's unwavering message was that each and every baby born is a clean slate: that peace on earth begins with birth; that each new life is a chance for humanity to achieve charitable greatness. In spite of the surfeit of record-smashing, culture-shaping career accolades Michael acquired, his only wish was to be remembered as an advocate for the children of the world. In the very month of his death, he said,

"That's what I'll be remembered for – not for what I did on stage, but for what I did for the children."

And in the same way Michael strived to defend the rights of children and promulgate the idea of the global resourcing of their innate genius, he felt that children were there to redeem him also, "I want to be buried right where there are children. I want them next to me. I would feel safer that way. I want them next to me. I need their spirit protecting me."

Had the *This Is It* endeavour proved successful, Michael would have earned over a billion dollars from ticket sales and merchandising. This figure in itself proves the tenacity of his legacy; how that even the most cynical can mature beyond their bitterness; and that eventually, everyone turns full circle - and in doing so - retrieves their fig leaf.

Perhaps the explanation for Michael's innate advocacy of childhood can be found through the fact that he grew up singing songs with lyrics such lyrics as, "With a child's heart / Nothing can ever get you down / With a child's heart / You've got no reason to frown", whilst simultaneously being abused behind the scenes. Perhaps it was a congenitally bestowed divine mission. To a large extent, the reason is irrelevant. What matters, is that his ethos of honouring the innocence of childhood continues to be promoted.

Both for Michael's sake, and our own.

CHAPTER EIGHT

As if you were on fire from within. The moon lives in the lining of your skin.

PABLO NERUDA

I once ran alone into the deserted streets of a small coastal town in the south of England, whereupon I tore off my shirt, fell to my knees, and wailed incoherently with primeval, ecstatic joy. Because a woman had just released fourteen white doves: one to represent each of Michael's acquittals in his 2005 trial for child molestation.

And, admittedly, that sounds like somewhat melodramatic behaviour. But it was an instinctive response. Such was Michael's touch.

I never met Michael. The closest I came to realising that oft-recurring dream was when I desperately clung onto the back of a car he'd just got in. Attached by mere fingertips, I bounced along behind the vehicle, with all the joy and manic apprehension of paraphernalia attached to the rear of a wedding car.

I can also lay claim to being the recipient of the gift of pizza and blankets from Michael, which he had sent to us whilst we waited outside a concert arena in sub-zero temperatures. It was acts of caring such as this delivery that became the reason why a teenage boy from the north of England covered his bedroom window with the words: MJ IS INNOCENT.

As well, having been a regular front-row concert attendee, I'm convinced I did once lock eyes with him: in Dublin, where it had still been daylight when the show started. I was certainly doing my bit to be noticed, anyway. To the extent where I imagine Michael might have been thinking, "Well, that's one I'm definitely staying away from." I also once caught the hat when it was thrown out during 'Billie Jean'. Before losing my grip in the ensuing ruckus.

It's easy to judge those of us that did things like that. But the euphoric frenzy the man inspired - the piquing of anticipation - was like nothing else. Michael's presence had a unique property: it osmotically transformed the atmosphere in a room - a change sensed by fan and non-fan alike (at least - you *used* to be a non-fan.) That very particular sense of butterflies in the stomach being simultaneously shared by thousands of people; with everyone feeling the experience as a reciprocated love for each other. It was inimitable.

Besides, Michael actively courted this fan reaction, even going so far as to endanger his own life in order to ignite such delirium, by standing on top of cars surrounded by thousands of baying fans.

Michael's long-time tour drummer, Jonathan 'Sugarfoot' Moffett, recalled,

"CNN said that over one billion people mourned Michael from all the remote areas of the world, as well as all the known areas. What other human being can draw that much sympathy and that much hurt from their loss. Michael had something special, a radiance, and when you were in his presence the whole room changed… Michael had the highest level of energy I think without being from another world. His gift and his humanity of spirit were just so powerful and great and deep. He was a different human being from most of us; from all of us. He did affect everybody that came around him, from leaders of the world to normal folk… Every single person that's been around him said they felt something, that I remember seeing or talking to… And that's why people cry. People absolutely cry. I would sit on stage and watch them pass bodies… You would see them lift bodies, arms dangling and legs, heads swinging, and there was like an ocean of people with their arms up passing bodies to the front, to the gate… One by one, people were passing them forward; sometimes a multitude of bodies moving across the crowd being passed to the rescue people… Some people were just totally gone, unconscious…

just from being in that stadium with Michael… It was just the most powerful thing to see, and that's just from that one man in the centre of the stage… He knew he was gifted with something special, a purpose; uniting the world and uniting people."

One of the many tragedies of Michael's death is the knowledge that we can never experience that feeling again. The last time I experienced it was at the O2 press conference that announced the *This Is It* venture. Though then, of course, the feeling was just one ingredient in a strange potion that also contained triumph and niggling concern.

***

How does one explain the magnetism of Michael? How so many are so heartbroken and mournful at the death of someone they never met - to the same extent of sadness that accompanies losing a close family member?

There are many reasons: Michael was an engine of pure prolificity in providing the world with quality, unique, timeless rhythms and melodies divined with purpose of healing the world; he was the plausible, flesh-and-blood superhero; he was a surrogate parent; he filled the vacuum of self for so many people confused by the tragedy of loss; he was the Unknown Soldier, with millions of identities willed onto him by the bereft.

The world talks about Michael Jackson as an unbreakable enigma. But he wasn't. Not to us. Not to those of us that walked through hell with him, its raging fires starkly illuminating the man's vulnerabilities and faults – for anyone that cared to see. What he gave us in return is this: he gave us musical flags to plant as life milestones - points of reference galvanized by the soul orgasm of zeitgeist; he was our support system; he was an indicator for our identities - our very souls; he was our moral paradigm, a totem for our tried-and-tested, stoic-and-steadfast belief in the power of the truth - in the indefatigable advocating of it when confronted by egregious, audacious and unrelenting slander.

Indeed, reading the salacious descriptions of Michael quoted by tabloids and their anonymous sources is akin to listening to someone detail the character of a mutual friend, a person you have known for decades, but who they have only recently become acquainted with. You know this old friend inside-out – their flaws, their tribulations, their virtues – and are therefore gobsmacked by the inaccuracy of this other person's depiction of them.

As Michael sang, "Your cameras can't control / The minds of those who know / That you'll even sell your soul / Just to get your story sold."

The fable of *Beauty and the Beast* tells the tale of how decency is perennially ostracised by the cynicism of a society obsessed with superficiality. How scapegoating, promoted by the insecurity of bullies fearful of deviants, manifests in the Beast as his becoming more and more isolated. The love story in the fable demonstrates how two people find solace in each other after this rejection from society. This is the same as between Michael and his fans. Michael would not give up because he had the love from his fans. And we would not, and will not, give up because we had his.

With the increasing brutality Michael endured, the more we were drawn to him. The poor black boy born as a single permutation of the infinity of fate into - to borrow Janet's phrase - "a world sick with racism", who went on to defy the odds by escaping poverty and using his sacrifice of self to influence and help transform the world into a better place.

And in this is where the most significant answer to the conundrum of the world's sense of grief at his death lies: simply, that the world is mourning en masse at the instinctive tragedy of our losing an opportunity for peace. As the musician Erykah Badu said: "He's in our DNA".

What kind of man inspires such depth of devotion where, in the absence of any official Mecca for their martyred hero, fans organise pilgrimages to the impenetrable gates of his house? What kind of man generates a loyalty entirely unfazed, infinite and unwavering, despite daily ad hominem attacks on him and his supporters? What kind of man invokes rapture at the slightest sight of his twitching a curtain? What kind of man enkindles vigils?

It is the kind of man who transformed the curse of a disease into a totem of equality; who - singlehandedly, using his unparalleled level of fame - attempted to undo centuries of blackface minstrel mockery of his race, yet not with a sense of vengeance, but with a motive for human unity; it is the kind of man who made a concerted effort to be Christ-like, who poured his wealth on the poor and emulated the children; it is the kind of man that taught us that perception is merely a reflection of oneself, that love is truth, and that sacrifice is something to aspire to.

Michael's mission stalled when, after perceived provocations, he was arrested, and his character assassinated. How Michael's message is interpreted is vitally important to humanity, considering the unique stature that lends itself to the totemic.

Michael always said it was his stature that made him such an easy target for the sheer volume and size of rocks that were thrown at him. But it is also this stature that enables his utilisation as a global symbol for love and peace. The attacks continue, of course. They will never let him rest in peace, which is why the fan community is so important. He rescued so many of our childhoods, and it's our duty to protect and defend him in his death. It is us, the fans, who must defend against the apparently compulsory attacks undertaken by those happy to be pseudo-educated by sensationalist tabloid headlines and Internet links.

Now. Wouldn't it be great if we could all get along in the fight against that?

The press are now more vulnerable in the wake of the Leveson enquiry. We will not stand idly by and watch Michael Jackson slandered. We will make a noise; we will raise our voice as one.

***

The loyalty of Michael's fans is akin to that within a family. A family such as the Jacksons themselves. Any large community is not only a reflection, but a macrocosm of the family condition, with the identifiable stereotypes that that contains: stoic matriarchs, scapegoated sons, reliable aunts, reclusive uncles, embarrassing patriarchs and vulnerable teenagers.

Out of this quagmire of inextricably linked characters and personality disorders emerges the ubiquitous backstabbing, name-calling and oneupmanship of human beings that know precisely which buttons to press in order to garner a reaction from their kin. What also emerges, however, is the unparalleled capacity for forgiveness, understanding and unwavering support in the face of cruel adversity. Such as being at your brother's side throughout a gruelling trial in which he is accused of molesting children.

The Jackson family, however, must not only deal with their own family dynamics, but also with being the projection screen for every angst-ridden fan with family rage as well; with online social networking meaning that they now have front row seats in their very own cinema of abuse. (And that's before you even consider the traditional buzz of irrational hatred aimed at the family that is stirred and perpetuated by tabloid press and television. But then, they're used to that.)

The Michael Jackson fan community is much less divided, as it is obliterated into smithereens; comprised, as it is, of as many factions as to rival the Christian church, with each cohort manipulating the belief system in a way to suit their specific requirements. And within a fanbase as vast as an artist such as Michael's is, it is right and inevitable that these variations will exist.

However, the proposed sale of Neverland is a rare opportunity for a united stance amongst Michael's fans, whose capacity for bickering amongst themselves is tantamount to self-sabotage. There has been enough rock-throwing. The philosopher Confucius contemplated that, at the point where one faction of a battle appears to be in control, the wisest thing to do is allow the opposition to retreat across their bridge, thus allowing them the opportunity of distance to reconsider their perspective. Certain factions of Michael's fan community have arrived at such a juncture.

One of the reasons it's so hard to consider the idea that fans in the opposing corner might be motivated by love, is because that would suggest that their opinions must therefore have credence. Yet, those two issues are entirely unrelated. A great deal of arguing just assumes the hate-based motivations of the other side as standard. The strategy in such opining is rarely to change enemies' perceptions. A project for change would surely be better advantaged by accepting the idea that those fans with opposing views also think of themselves as decent, loving people. When you believe your enemies are also galvanised by love, it must be more likely that a compromise can be reached. You don't need to like your opponent - let alone acquiesce to their argument - in order to understand that they really like themselves, and that this liking of themselves probably means more to *them* than does their disliking of you.

Progress in resolving conflicts within the fan community will only come about when we all understand that the love each and every one of has for Michael is sincere, regardless of which pane of the prism we peer at him through. Michael effortlessly inspires sincerity.

As Michael sang, "This is our mission, to see it through / This is our planet, you're one of us / "You're just another part of me" – we're just another part of each other, with Michael as a conduit.

Michael holds up a mirror to humanity. His fans were given the opportunity to perceive the world through his own particular pane of the prism: one painful, yet privileged. Each of us fans as individuals is in some way a reflection of the man himself, with his common goal:

to help heal the world. Those who project themselves onto Michael and see a monster are merely construing themselves. The only monster is the one interpreted. There is no evidential basis whatsoever for a belief in Michael as a monster. It was envy and extortionists that did that. As Michael sang, "The heart reveals the proof / Like a mirror reveals the truth."

If I could wish for anything, it would be that everyone could perceive Michael the way we do, regardless of our political stance.

The Estate of Michael Jackson is being sued for their attempted deceit of fans. This is a prime opportunity for the millions of fans seduced by the capitalist mutation offered by the Estate as a replacement idol, to evolve in the same way that Michael did: from the man obsessed with having the world's biggest selling record, to the man obsessed with building the world's biggest children's hospital; from materialism to spiritualism. Our peaceful protest in defending the legacy and name of Michael Jackson is gathering pace. Our numbers are amassing. Recruits are being educated with the knowledge that a life of the magnitude of Michael Jackson's cannot be frittered away by those motivated by mindless greed and vacuous consumerism. Michael Jackson's life is a chance for the people of the planet to reflect upon what is actually important for each and every one of us. And I don't imagine media-driven malice is high up there on that list.

The perpetuation of the lie of Michael being a child molester undermines his life's work, his message and his mission. This is the single issue, above all others, which is the most crucial with regards Michael's legacy. To fight against this, we can disregard our other differences. This is the true cause that unites the Michael Jackson fan community.

Indeed, if the success of a leader is measured by the loyalty of his followers, there is none stronger than Michael, regardless of which faction of fans you might represent. Michael refused to change direction with his beliefs. And we must remain just as unwavering in our defence of him. We must remain fortitudinous in the fulfilling of his mission: each of us taking pride in our position as a requisite speck of light on the peacock's coalescent coat, in order that we contribute to its immortality. And that we do so – in triumph.

'Murmuration' is the word given to the spectacle of flocking starlings (the avian visual antithesis to the peacock) as they pulsate in unified splendour. As the starlings chirp and whistle, as they coalesce in open skies, they bring to mind the words of our artist - that "there's nothing that can't be done, if we raise our voice as one." Murmuration is a phenomenon observed at dusk, as starlings prepare to roost.

Conversely, however - as one UK tabloid recently noted in response to a fan anti-defamation campaign - "the Michael Jackson fans are just waking up."

***

Michael performed to hundreds of millions of people during his life. Every crowd he played to was comprised of an adoring ocean of people, in which each individual had fallen as a nuanced raindrop, forming a harmonious sea of love: a form that was fluid, yet entire – like the dancer and the dance that had summoned them all to be together. And Michael gleefully received this love. More than that: he was energised by it. Arms outstretched, awash in the pulsing warmth of the love of a hundred-thousand people, he absorbed the adoration the way a butterfly imbues heat – in order to generate enough strength to fly.

When on tour, Michael would scream to the sound engineers, "Hurt me!" in a request for them to increase the volume and intensity of the music. And indeed there was a sense of the masochist in his work ethic. The global events that were Michael Jackson World Tours caused him renewed suffering from various medical conditions. The poor state of his lungs – likely a consequence of the merciless schedule thrust upon him as a child that involved singing nightly in the smoky venues the *Jackson 5* played (oh the irony of that word!).

During parts of the *Dangerous* tour, Michael was so ill he was sometimes having to exit the stage mid-song in order to take oxygen. With this borne in mind, then, the efforts exerted in his planetary crisscrossing - as courageous as they would be even for someone in their physical prime - become viewed as being nothing short of superhuman.

As Michael's health deteriorated, so conversely increased the intensification of his efforts to relay, promote and safeguard his message of peace.

The ecstasy Michael experiences during the Wembley *Bad* tour performance of 'I Just Can't Stop Loving You', as the crowd sings those very words to him, is starkly evident. The *Bad* album was conceived from the very first as a stadium record, with the songs intended to be brought to life on stages across the world. And it's no coincidence that Michael hands the microphone over to the audience for the chorus in 'I Just Can't Stop Loving You', before explicitly, passionately imploring the crowd to, "Tell me! Tell me!"

There are many instances that showboat Michael's capacity for generalising songs from his personal experience into a broader theme. In 'I Just Can't Stop Loving You', Michael sings that "Love is the answer… / This thing can't go wrong…/ We can change all the world tomorrow." Whilst in 'Give in to Me', his covert message to the world was, "It seems you get your kicks from hurting me…You and your friends were laughing at me in town… You won't be laughing, when I'm not around".

And truly, we are not.

Michael had been conditioned from a very young age to believe in a correlation between the volume of the ovation he received from an audience and the amount of love he deserved. During the twenty years between the record-breaking *Bad* Tour of 1988 and the ill-fated swansong of 2009, the set-list of his concerts and its choreography rarely strayed from the iconic hits of *Thriller* and *Bad*. These were the songs of his hey-day, and so, naturally, were also the songs in which he received the loudest ovations. Michael needed to feel our love. Visitors to Neverland speak of the ranch as brimming with gifts from fans - a veritable hoarder's paradise. Each cherished by Michael as a token of love for him.

And he needs that now more than ever.

***

When I was sixteen, I boarded a coach, upon which I sat for thirty hours, before disembarking in Prague in the Czech Republic. As a painfully shy teenager, I wasn't confident enough to be forthright enough to make friends on the journey, so the trip was undertaken alone. Besides, I wasn't travelling to make friends. I was going to see Michael. I hadn't seen him for four years, since that soul-altering night on the *Dangerous* tour. I was nauseous with excitement.

It was so cold. But I was determined to get a position close to the front of the following day's concert, so, after being stood a short while at the feet of the specially erected Stalin-esque *HIStory* statue - staring up at it, both bewildered and awestruck - I left the coach party. After mindlessly navigating the streets of the alien city for a number of hours, I eventually managed to stumble across the stadium, Letna Park; where I joined a throng of similarly single-minded diehards who were also gathering to queue overnight before the concert. But it was so cold.

The concert happened. I had managed to hold my own in the downright dangerous race to the front, once the gates finally opened. And - devoid of food and sleep - had also, somehow, managed to stay vertical all day, in spite of the intermittent tidal surges created by the momentum transfer of one-hundred-and-thirty-thousand people (the largest live crowd Michael ever performed to) standing behind me.

As well as when we all jumped and joined along together in singing, "Tom Sneddon is a cold man."

I filled my pockets with the confetti that had burst from cannons signalling the end of the show, then – very, very slowly – shuffled my way to a merchandise tent. My understanding of the Czech currency was limited at best, and my adrenaline was sky-high: a combination ripe for disaster. The kind of disaster where you find yourself lost and alone, at night, in the middle of a mid-nineties, recently Eastern Bloc capital city wearing the three Michael Jackson T-shirts you've just spent all your money on, whilst also clutching the tour programme as close to your torso as possible, in an attempt to achieve that extra microtherm of warmth.

I had a ticket with the name of the hotel I was supposed to be staying in, but I couldn't pronounce its name, and the odd person that walked past who I summoned the courage to engage and show the ticket to, just shrugged at me and continued walking. After the roar of the concert, everything seemed more silent than was possible.

Penniless on the deserted streets of Prague, I sat down and cried. Then a car pulled up.

A woman wound down the window and garbled something in a foreign language, whilst gesturing for me to approach her. She was my only hope. I showed her the ticket. Again, a shrug and a look of confusion. My heart sank as I was hit with a genuine terror that I wasn't going to be either home, warm, eating or sleeping any time soon. Then the woman, whose face had empathetically mirrored my own as it fell, suddenly pointed at my T-shirt (the top one, anyway), and simply said, "Michael!", before directing me to take a seat in the back of the car, and beginning to drive around what came to seem like endless, dark, desolate city streets. Finally, she turned a corner, and I saw something I recognised. Illuminated like a homing beacon, in all its elucidated glory, stood the *HIStory* statue.

And at its feet, my ride home.

The closing words to Michael's song 'The Lost Children' are uttered by his own children, and are of them recognising that it's time to return home, as it's getting dark.

As many of us do when we're feeling lost, I simply had to return to Michael; to the light.

***

There is a photograph of me as an eleven-year-old boy, in which I am stood proudly in front of one of the walls of my bedroom. Behind me, each and every inch of the wall is plastered in pictures of Michael in various poses: most of them of him on stage wearing either the silver shirt from the *Bad* tour or the gold leotard from the *Dangerous* tour. Some of the pictures are huge, one of them is as small as a postage stamp (for those pesky spaces adjacent to light switches - I would have bought an entire magazine solely for that picture). The other walls, the ones not featured in the photograph, were adorned in the same way. As was the ceiling. My younger brother and I shared the bedroom, and one of our favourite things to do was agree to intermittently rearrange our pictures. It would take us entire weekends.

This photograph is over two decades old now. It is beginning to brown around the edges. My memories of those times are often played on Super 8 film. There is a yellow saturation to them, and its inhabitants move with a strange and erratic jerkiness; a dreamlike dance akin to how toddlers dart around. The photographs evoke a sense of nostalgia that invokes a spirit of eighties and early nineties summers; of hotplate patio flags and the riled ants that filed from the cracks between them; of music from a far off radio somehow managing to carry all the poignancy of a Muezzin's call to prayer, as it infused thermal air currents with otherworldliness. Radios that would, naturally, have been playing Michael's music.

No-one embodies the zeitgeist of those years better than Michael. I sometimes experience waves of Michael-specific nostalgia inspired by a mere scent or particular lighting. In an instant I can be stood in the queue waiting for the coach to take me to my first concert: *Dangerous* tour, Roundhay Park, Leeds, August 16th 1992. I was twelve.

Pre-Internet, we had pen pals that sent us cassettes and VHS tapes that were ultimately played to ruin. Cassettes containing *The Jacksons* album, with rarities such as 'The Man' or 'Whatzupwitu' tagged onto the end, to fill up the space. Our longplay version of *MTV*'s 'Dangerous Diaries' was our most prized possession. Those tapes contained a lot of soul. The Holy Grail was a *Victory* tour performance or *Bad* tour second leg concert on VHS. We finally received the latter in 2012 as part of the *Bad 25* anniversary package (with the Estate's profiteers even being kind enough to retain the same levels of quality control exhibited by those mail-order bootlegs from back in the day).

My Michael nostalgia begins in 1987. But imagine those fans that saw that unique star as it began to twinkle in that coruscant dusk of 1969 – then followed its celestial trajectory all the way through to the dark dawn of 2009? That's a whole gamut of Michael zeitgeist.

The analogy of Michael's lifetime being a nighttime is an interesting one. Michael always said that he was merely a conduit for the wishes of a higher being, such as how the moon is to the sun. The moon reflects light from the sun, which illuminates our darkness when the sun is not around, and in much the same way, Michael lit up the darker occasions of many of our lives. In turn, those that support and honour him, borrow light from him also.

There is a faction of fans that call themselves 'Moonwalkers'. The original name for the dance-move now universally recognised as the 'Moonwalk', was the rather insipid, 'backslide'. Michael premiered the move on *Motown 25*: the show, which - fittingly - fired him into the stratosphere and transformed him into the most luminous superstar the planet had ever seen. Michael's sincere intent and corresponding actions in changing the world for the better began on that night, and continued for the remainder of his corporeal existence. It's up to all fans - Moonwalkers *et al* - to help ensure this continues.

In the song 'Cry', the call-and-response between Michael and God illustrates Michael's self-awareness of his mission perfectly: the closing words being Michael's (or is it God's?) instruction to "change the world". Now Michael is gone, the call-and-response can even be interpreted as Michael talking to each and every one of his fans. Since Michael's death, to quote St. Teresa of Avila, his fans "…are the eyes with which he looks with compassion on this world". 'Cry' has become the anthem for 'World Cry Day', marked by fans on 25 June - the anniversary of Michael's passing.

***

There's a system of belief in which the idea is promoted that human beings, in-between our earthly existences, gather together with all the souls we are bound to encounter in our next corporeal adventure. The night of August 28th, 1958 must have been quite the event.

The subsequent day, Katherine Jackson gave birth to her eighth child. Another boy. Her mother suggested she named him 'Ronald'. Katherine - thankfully - ignored that, and opted for 'Michael' - after the patron saint of soldiers. A name that means "Who is like God".

Maybe at that pre-terrestrial meeting, Michael signed up for a corporeal life of sacrifice. That he courageously adopted the responsibility of being a messenger to attempt to guide humanity along a more peaceful path.

This theory is something of a consolation when recalling the quagmire of sufferance Michael's life became. As an erudite human being brought up in a Christian household, it's impossible to consider that parallels between himself and Jesus Christ did not occur to him. Indeed – again, much to his critical detriment – Michael actively marketed Christ's message to a capitalist society through his performances of 'Earth Song' at the *Brits '96* (recently voted the greatest *Brits* performance of all time) and again later the same year at the *World Music Awards*.

In the *HIStory* track 'Tabloid Junkie' Michael even sings, "…with your pen you torture men / You'd crucify the Lord."

It is a travesty that the triumvirate of topics that people discuss regarding Michael does not automatically include his humanitarian efforts. Above all else, this should be the overarching one – the trinity that coalesces as one.

Love survives. It is forever. From the physical ecstasy married with the discovery of true love, to the spiritual repercussions found in a steadfast love that has matured, fortified and been vindicated by faith.

As Michael mused,

"Hope is such a beautiful word, but it often seems very fragile. Life is still being needlessly hurt and destroyed. Because I believe the answer to be faith; not hope."

Yet, our stance on Michael's message and his innocence is not about mere angles of moral perspective. It is about defending the reputation of an inordinately good man – in light of the facts, not faith.

***

The silent pilot light of achieving one's aspirations flickers persistently throughout an entire lifetime, though the cynicism of society relentlessly attempts to extinguish the flame. This self-sabotaging phenomenon is fuelled by an ubiquitous misbelief amongst the embittered, of their having missed the opportunity to fulfil their own dreams. This byproduct of envy is not the fault of those afflicted, however: more a logical consequence of the inherent difficulty in leaping over the ego and reacquainting themselves with the indomitable optimism embodied by their inner child.

Fortunate people are blessed with having had faith instilled within themselves. This fortune is derived from the quality of being enlightened recipients of unconditional love and support. The peerless strength that comes with possessing an innate knowledge of being loved is what imbues the requisite confidence and courage vital for remaining stoic in actively advocating the validity of one's intuited belief system, regardless of the bombardment of a sneering society.

The pilot light of aspiration remains until a person's dying day. During a lifetime, there are intermittent instances of inhaling breaths of inspiration that when exhaled potentiate the luminescence of the flame. As an elucidated entity of being loved, a person is accordingly bestowed with the self-belief that is required for the courage to follow the flame.

We have arrived at such an instance. As Michael's fans, every single one of us is loved unconditionally (let's call it an occupational perk). Ergo, our collective inhalation of inspired breath, upon being exhaled, carries the potency required to combust Michael's pilot light dream of a universally recognised reverence for childhood, into an incendiary reality.

As fans, it is our responsibility to ensure that the sadness Michael was forced to endure makes sense in the end. That it meant something. Let us not allow the phenomenon that was Michael Jackson be a missed opportunity for an ambassador; an emblem; a paradigm of peace. Who knows when – or if – the world will ever know again anyone so universally recognised, whose sole intention was to help humanity evolve from its ubiquitous acts of bestial violence, and towards universally practiced ideals of peace? Michael encouraged the people of planet Earth to adopt his unprecedented fame and utilise it as a chance for global unity: as a catalyst for the positive progression of the human race. His life was one of self-sacrifice for our entertainment – it being the inimitable tragedy of Shakespearean proportions that it was.

Surely, the fulfilment of Michael's wish of him being a totem for love and understanding is not merely one he earnestly deserved, but one the world should be emphatically embracing? Or at least be grateful that he granted us the chance? People underestimate the fact that Michael was the most famous person on planet Earth. A heavy fact with unimaginable repercussions for the man. One day, people will envy our privilege as having been upon the same planet as a living Michael Jackson: a man that tried to teach that life itself is legacy; a man who endorsed the idea that each human being needs to care deeply about what happens to the next generation, and that this crucial wisdom for humanity's future must be instilled in people as children. As the little girl's voice that introduces 'Heal The World' states, "Think about the generations… they want to make the world a better place – for our children, and our children's children."

History is a weapon in the battle for objectivity. Michael understood this (it's an omnipresent motivational factor in the daily lives of his fans that now continuously defend him in the face of relentless attempts to bastardise his very own history. Even, seemingly, by those currently occupying the helm of his Estate).

The Arab Spring that began in 2010 demonstrated the incredible power to create positive change that lies patiently poised within postmodern media practices. The bestial vindictiveness that is the predictable backlash from traditional media outlets attempting to nullify these occurrences is something that Michael fought in the face of, every day. Michael was the magnetic musician of the people, a musical angel who defied expectations thrust upon him by this close-minded media. He challenged them, and in doing so, sacrificed his life. We must make the most of the bittersweet fruits borne of a uniquely oppressed childhood and subsequently misunderstood adulthood. We must undo the damage done by the demonic. We must be brave in outing and ousting the bullies. We owe it to Michael. We owe it to his mission. In the developed world, children have been removed from workhouses and relieved of their yokes, and have been granted rights instead. Michael is a catalyst for this achievable ideal to be made the norm across the entire globe. Michael could see that the time and technology was imminent for the mass utilisation of free information and communication for the doing of good. Michael was a man worth believing in; Michael was a visionary; Michael was a prophet.

We must incorporate arguments such as those contained within this book into Michael's legacy. So that the truth and the love survives, regardless of the bombardment of greed it has to endure by the unscrupulous nature of the people currently at the helm. One of my main motivations for writing this book was to assist in ensuring that there is something out there, somewhere, that exposes both the extent of Michael's genius and how he chose to utilise it for an intent of such purity, regardless of an attempted weathering of it motivated by myriad reasons. Michael's legacy will endure to legend. The only question is what the myths entwined within that legend will entail. This book is an effort to balance the legend in Michael's favour:

ballast that counters the attempted promulgation of him as a pop caricature, and promotes him as a prophet.

Prior to Neverland and Michael's attempt at creating a safe haven for innocence; prior to the *Pepsi* promo burning incident (occurring on the exact middle day of his life) that introduced him to the ephemeral relief of prescription painkillers; prior to the mass media opprobrium; prior to the child molestation allegations, Michael was interviewed candidly in the gardens of the Encino family home. The interview was later commercially released, much to his dismay. In said video, dubbed *Unauthorised,* Michael is seen crooning at the night sky – astonished, inspired and bewildered by the beauty of it all. High on nature and his unique connection to its elements, he feels he can fly, and dances as if he's a bird taking flight. Or, perhaps – a butterfly.

Michael's lifelong martyrdom ensured that he earned those wings.

And though the sun may set – remember, we glow by the moon.

AFTERWORD

One of the many things that Michael said which has stuck with me, was how he spoke of his admiration for people that used their talents to further the prospects of children. This is what I aspire to do.

My ambition as a writer is to help enrich the lives of children. As well as my writings on Michael, I am also a children's author. I have written a biography on Michael Jackson, and my hope is that I can utilise the success of the book to generate publicity for my children's books. They are written in the spirit of Michael, and as such, I will be donating a percentage of all sales to the non-profit organisation, Michael Jackson's Legacy (http://www.michaeljacksonslegacy.org).

More works from Syl Mortilla coming very soon.

ACKNOWLEDGEMENTS

I always assumed that by the point I'd got to the Acknowledgements section, I'd be delirious with relief; what with it being the ultimate full-stop. The reality is hitherto inexperienced levels of anxiety upon emancipating these words from the security of my computer and into the world of critical analysis.

This book is the product of the accumulated knowledge of twenty-five years of fanhood. A fanhood like no other with regards the extent of ad hominem opprobrium suffered by its membership. I'd like to thank every member of our much-maligned community who has stood up and been counted in our fight to defend our hero's legacy.

Special thanks go to my friend and agent Samar Habib, for his unwavering support - both practically, in his proofreading and cover design capabilities, as well as spiritually, in his capacity to inspire and encourage. Indeed, the very first blog post that formed the foundations for this book was borne as a result of his encouragement.

Similarly, I must thank Christina Drake – her wisdom and unrelenting faith in my ambitions as a writer have been crucial in the production of this book. I love you.

It's difficult to express the immense gratitude I have for Karen Faye, Harrison Funk and Lena Wilson as to their contributions in making my book look so beautiful and lending my words such credence. I am indebted. Thank you to you all for your kindness, and for inspiring me with the bravery of honesty. To Karen, for your recommendation that Michael never did things by halves.

I have many, many people to thank for helping me write this book:

My brother, Andrew, who started it all with that *Thriller* cassette.

People who have afforded me their time in proofreading: Thomas Hannan; Jessica Lockyear.

People who have afforded me food whilst I obstinately refused to acquiesce to full time employment: Mum and Dad; Gran and Grandad; Thomas Hannan; Jessica Lockyear; Sarah Tymms; Peter Mills; Phil Rust; Charlie Thomson.

Charlie Thomson once again, for your caring - and also to the rest of the MJFU crew for their intelligence, objectivity, and insults. What a family.

MJFU individuals in particular: Morganna Bramah; Sandra "Furnace" De La Vega Anderson (and her MJTalks ladies); Mari Belfort; Daniel Skinner; Ryan Michaels; Amanda Mands; Alexei Penfold.

Alexei Penfold once again, for your illustrative work when I was trying to find a cover design. The same goes for Karin Merx – thank you so much for the time and effort you put in. Your illustrations were beautiful, I hope they come in useful one day. Thanks also to Karin's colleagues at MJAS.

Fellow blogger Damien Shields and the A Truth Untold team.

***

Each and every time my daughters asked me to stay and play with them, and I had to tell them that I had to leave as I was writing a book, it splintered my heart. They saw my hesitance in having to go, but told me it was fine - so long as I promised to write them a letter to include in the book:

Dear Myla and Sylva,

This book is about the potency of faith and dreams; how the silent pilot light of potentiating one's aspirations persists throughout an entire lifetime. It is about the fragility of human nature, with one of its consequences being that other people will attempt to extinguish the flame.

Though no-one does this with an innate malicious intent. It is due to an all-too common and tragic belief held by some that they have missed the opportunity to fulfil their own dreams. This sorrowful mindset is made manifest through expressions the very antithesis of faith and dreams: envy and cynicism. Evil does not exist, only lack of love. Bombard any situation with patient love and anything will heal.

Fortunate people are blessed with having had faith instilled with themselves. I have entire faith in you. This quality of being a recipient of unconditional love and support is the very essence of this book. It is about actively advocating the validity of your intuited belief system, regardless of any perceived detriment. Either to others or yourself. The most natural thing in the world is to understand what the right thing to do is, yet apprehensively opt in delaying to act upon its truth. Everyone's dreams of contentment are different, but whatever yours may be, make sure you take them by the scruff of their necks and drag them into reality. As Charles Dickens wrote, "'Procrastination is the thief of time, collar him.'

The pilot light remains until your dying day. During your time of being alive, there are frequent instances of inhaling an inspiration that when exhaled would potentiate the luminescence of the flame. Life is about learning to recognise these moments whilst possessing a capacity for self-belief that bestows enough courage to follow the flame. The fire will not always combust to a satisfactorily spectacular level. Because life is also about perseverance and industry. Acquiring the requisite level of fitness to exhale purposely enough to embolden the pilot light in order to illuminate it to its perfect potential requires training. You must work at your craft. But to succeed it must be a craft that excites your heart. There will be lulls. They will provoke doubt and anxiety. But you know what you're good at. And don't let anyone dictate otherwise.

With such a profound and infinite love that is inherently impossible to express in words,

Daddy.

Printed in Great Britain
by Amazon.co.uk, Ltd.,
Marston Gate.